Praise for How to Be Brilliant at Public Speaking

'In her book *How to Brilliant at Public Speaking* Sarah Lloyd-Hughes shares secrets of success that it has taken me many years to learn as an experienced public speaker. Packed with humour, easy to use practical tips from experts, case stories and much more, Sarah's book will teach you all you need to authentically and powerfully connect with any audience.'

Steven D'Souza, Executive Fellow IE Business School, Author *Brilliant Networking*, www.brilliantnetworking.net

'A must-buy for nervous beginners and more experienced speakers alike. This comprehensive guide to public speaking is presented in an easily digested and friendly format – great to duck in and out of when you need it. With experience, wit and intelligence, Sarah Lloyd-Hughes shows you how you can be a great speaker, without sacrificing your authenticity.

If you want to be brilliant at public speaking – this is the best possible place to start.'

Nigel Risner, motivational speaker and author of *It's a Zoo Around Here*. Former Speaker of the Year - The Academy of Chief Executives and The Executive Committee

'Becoming great at presenting is so very important for being visible and getting ahead in business today. This wonderful book provides you with all the tools you need to succeed when on your feet in front of an audience. I shall certainly be recommending it to my clients.'

Lesley Everett, Personal Branding expert, speaker and author of *Drop Dead Brilliant*

'Sarah has written an outstanding book. She has taken what can be a daunting topic, broken it down into bite-sized chunks and then used fantastic drawings, analogies, characters and examples to get the message across. As a professional speaker of many years, I only wish this book had been around when I started out.'

David Thomas – *Sunday Times* **number one bestselling author, international speaker, Memory Champion and Guinness Record Breaker**

'The best possible introduction to public speaking, and it doesn't involve making yourself into someone you're not. Sarah shows you how to be an authentically powerful speaker who can command the room yet keep the stillness within – a rare combination.'

Tom Butler-Bowdon, author of 50 Self-Help Classics, 50 Psychology Classics, www.Butler-Bowdon.com

'The best book on public speaking I've ever read. With clarity and humour, Sarah Lloyd-Hughes offers invaluable insight, suggestions and tips. This is a wonderful book, bringing a fresh and light-hearted approach to the often fraught world of public speaking.'

Karen Kimsey-House, CEO and Co-founder, Coaches Training Institute and author of Co-active Coaching

'Enlightening, insightful and savvy – this book is packed with brilliant ideas to take you to the next level in the area of speaking. Probably one of the most clear, concise and useful books I have ever read on the subject.'

Paul McGee, 'The Sumo Guy' – one of the UK's leading business motivation speakers; Managing Director, PMA International Ltd

How to Be Brilliant at Public Speaking

Prentice Hall LIFE

If life is what you make it, then making it better starts here.

What we learn today can change our lives tomorrow. It can change our goals or change our minds; open up new opportunities or simply inspire us to make a difference. That's why we have created a new breed of books that do more to help you make more of *your* life.

Whether you want more confidence or less stress, a new skill or a different perspective, we've designed *Prentice Hall Life* books to help you to make a change for the better. Together with our authors we share a commitment to bring you the brightest ideas and best ways to manage your life, work and wealth.

In these pages we hope you'll find the ideas you need for the life *you* want. Go on, help yourself.

It's what you make it

* * *

How to Be Brilliant at Public Speaking

Any audience. Any situation.

SARAH LLOYD-HUGHES

Prentice Hall Life
is an imprint of

Harlow, England • London • New York • Boston • San Francisco • Toronto • Sydney • Singapore • Hong Kong
Tokyo • Seoul • Taipei • New Delhi • Cape Town • Madrid • Mexico City • Amsterdam • Munich • Paris • Milan

PEARSON EDUCATION LIMITED

Edinburgh Gate
Harlow CM20 2JE
Tel: +44 (0)1279 623623
Fax: +44 (0)1279 431059
Website: www.pearson.com/uk

First published in Great Britain in 2011

Pearson Education is not responsible for the content of third-party internet sites.

ISBN: 978-0-273-75521-0

British Library Cataloguing-in-Publication Data
A catalogue record for this book is available from the British Library

Library of Congress Cataloging-in-Publication Data
Lloyd-Hughes, Sarah.
  How to be brilliant at public speaking : any audience, any situation / Sarah Lloyd-Hughes.
    p. cm.
  ISBN 978-0-273-75521-0 (pbk.)
  1. Public speaking. I. Title.
  PN4129.15.L65 2011
  808.5'1--dc23
                          2011027687

10 9 8 7 6 5
15 14 13

Cartoon illustrations by Sarah Lloyd-Hughes

Typeset in 9.5/13pt IowanOldBT by 30
Printed in Malaysia, CTP-PJB

Contents

Part 1 Awareness

The foundations of excellent speaking. Get rid of your speaking quirks and step into powerful expression.

Part 2 Empathy

Gain the respect of your audience by focusing on their needs.

Part 3 Freshness

Create memorable public speaking experiences with creative content.

Part 4 Balance

Develop structures that are powerful and aid your memory.

Part 5 Fearlessness

Part 6 Authenticity

About the author

Sarah Lloyd-Hughes, founder of Ginger Training & Coaching, is an experienced, energetic and empowering speaker, coach and writer who works with individuals to support them in reaching their potential. She has taught thousands of people of all ages across three continents. Ranging from professionals in India's largest IT company, to young people in inner-city London, Sarah builds confidence and inspiration in her audiences, whatever their experience levels.

Sarah's much-lauded workshops are bursting with fun, practical and extremely powerful ways to improve your public speaking. These days she focuses on working with professionals wishing to become key people of influence in their field. She challenges and supports them on the journey to become passionate, authentic and inspiring speakers.

A practising Buddhist, Sarah suffers from a lifelong obsession with happiness. Her personal passions include helping people 'live life outside the box', watching sunrise and eating cake whilst it's still warm.

For more information, please visit www.gingerpublicspeaking.com.

Acknowledgements

This book has been years in the making, but just a few intense months in the writing. It's not possible to count all the kind words, snippets of advice and gentle shoves that have contributed to its creation – thank you to all who provided them. But for reasons of practicality, I'd like to turn the spotlight on some of the contributors who have meant the most to me during this time.

My thanks must start at the beginning of my public speaking journey with the tremendous organisation that is AIESEC UK. Thank you for giving me that gut-wrenching experience of my very first speech. To this day, you continue to give young people outstanding opportunities to learn and grow.

Thanks to all of the experts who have contributed their time and wisdom to this project: thank you to the countless wonderful people who have helped me start my company, Ginger Training & Coaching, without whom I wouldn't be living my dream. My clients and fellow coaches and speakers are a constant source of learning and inspiration. James, Mara, Joel – thank you for giving me the confidence to believe that my silly little doodles (featured in this book) were worthy of public viewing.

My advisors, particularly Tom Butler-Bowden, Taz Miah and Adam Penny – thanks for your intelligent and sensible words and encouragement.

Jacqueline Burns of the Expert Agency, my wise and feisty agent – thank you so much for making all of this happen.

To my wonderful teachers who guide my desire to be beneficial in the world – a heartfelt thank you.

A final group, who perhaps should have been first. Thank you to my core of support as a coach, writer and human being – my ever-supportive mum, dad and brother, Lyndsay, Richard and James, for giving me so much self-confidence over the years. And thank you to my darling Lukasz for putting up with me and being my cheerleader when my head was stuck in a laptop for weeks on end.

To you, the reader, thanks for stopping by and I hope you benefit immensely from these words and ideas.

Introduction

Imagine you've just finished an important piece of public speaking. It went better than you could have ever dreamed. Your audience are beaming at you and you know that you hit the nail on the head. Everyone in the room leaves feeling more knowledgeable, inspired and ready for action.

This is closer to reality than you might think.

Yet, if you feel anything like I did when I first started speaking, it will seem like miles off. I remember watching those 'natural born public speakers' – people who just appear to leap up on stage and say the right thing at the right time. It seemed to me like they had a magic gene that allowed them to razzle dazzle their audience with their intelligence, humour and charm. And then when I thought of myself speaking, I felt like I was surrounded by neon lights telling everyone just how terrible I was.

It's easy to believe that you're the only one who's ever felt intimidated by public speaking. It's easy to focus on all those speakers who seem effortlessly to impress. And it's easy to silently protest, 'But I don't have anything to say', or 'Why would anyone listen to me?' or 'I just can't do it!' But you're not the first – or the last – public speaker to have those worries.

Beyond all proportion, public speaking is quoted as one of the most feared activities in the modern world. As Jerry Seinfeld famously quipped, 'to the average person, if you go to a funeral, you're better off in the casket than doing the eulogy.'

Although we hold a myth that in public speaking you either 'have it or you don't', there's really *no such thing as a natural born public speaker* ... just as there's no such thing as a natural born judo master, chess champion, accountant or any other expert.

The secret is that those 'naturally masterful' speakers have put in an enormous amount of time and positive effort to get where they are. They started where you are and they've battled their own fears, they've scratched their heads about what to speak about and they've pushed themselves beyond what they thought possible. The results can knock the socks off an audience.

So there's no reason why you can't do the same.

In fact, anyone who can carry a conversation can be a brilliant public speaker. How can I be so sure? Because I've come through it myself.

When I stepped out to deliver my first *ever* public speech, it was with the aim of convincing 200 people I should be chosen for my then dream job. It was a gut-wrenching experience, but I did it because I cared more about the dream job than my sweaty palms, my dry throat and my jelly legs. As I walked through the crowd to the stage, I had no idea whether a single word would come out.

Yet these days, people say these sorts of things about my speaking:

Sarah is outstanding on stage. She's riotously fun, totally engaging, experienced and inspiring.

Inspiring, passionate – watching Sarah in action is an affirming and empowering experience.

Sarah is a fantastic presenter and teacher. Watch her, learn from her and your public speaking will benefit.

How is such a difference possible if good speakers are born that way? It wasn't that (distinctly average) three-minute speech that revolutionised my public speaking, although I *did* get the job. Over time I developed techniques to get over the parts of public speaking that I found difficult. I learned how to tame my nerves, the best way to structure what I was saying, how to create an on-stage character that my audience enjoyed, and so on.

I learned that there are three secrets of public speaking:

Public speaking secret 1:
Anyone can learn to speak in public.
Public speaking secret 2:
Public speaking is an art, not a science.
Public speaking secret 3:
You already have everything you need to be a brilliant speaker.

Let's look at each of these principles in turn.

Public speaking secret 1: Anyone can learn to speak in public

You can never predict who the great public speakers in a room are, so I've stopped trying. I've seen shy introverts step onto stage and blow everyone away with powerful words and I've seen bouncy extroverts mumble and splutter until nobody in the audience is left listening. Public speaking is not about your personality, it's a skill that we can all learn.

The process of learning to speak in public is exactly the same as any other learning process. It will happen naturally, so long as you're willing to be brave and try something different. The key with public speaking is not to excuse yourself from it simply because you're nervous. Nerves are normal. Instead, progress little by little by stepping onto the **Learning Pathway**:

1. **Blissfully Unaware:** Most speakers who don't look for help are completely unaware of what they don't know. They're satisfied with their own performance, but from the audience's perspective they make lots of embarrassing mistakes because they don't have the skills to speak well.

2. **Rude Awakening:** As you read this book you may start to notice what you do that isn't as good as it could be. You see the gap between your abilities and where you'd like them to be. It can be difficult to hear, but the Rude Awakening is crucial to help you progress. If you don't have a single Rude Awakening during this book, then either you're a perfect speaker, or you haven't been honest with yourself.

3. **Awkward Ability:** Then, as you pick up some techniques, you'll start to put them into practice. This phase is like learning to drive – you're changing the gears, but you have to think about it to get it right. You will see that you're improving, but you may feel rather self-conscious in the process.

4. **Absorbed Expertise:** With time and practice a new behaviour will become a natural part of your public speaking that you're no longer aware of. It feels great to perform like an expert without even realising it. Then it's time to pick the next bit of your performance to work on.

Anyone who continues along the learning pathway for long enough and follows the techniques outlined in this book will become not just a competent speaker, but a brilliant speaker. The difference between those who make it and those who stop half-way is their reaction during the Rude Awakening and Awkward Ability phases. At these stages your confidence can take a dip as you realise you have work to do to improve your public speaking. It's by pushing through these difficult moments that you'll learn how to inspire others.

Public speaking secret 2: Public speaking is an art, not a science

A lot of the information we are fed as nervous or improving public speakers is about what we *should* and *shouldn't* be doing. Often experienced speakers share their anecdotes about what has worked for them and present them as a fact – 'Copy me and you'll be a successful speaker.' This makes it seem like there is a science to speaking well.

In my experience, this is misleading for two reasons. First, remembering all of the rules of what you *should* and *shouldn't* be doing makes you *more* nervous, rather than less. Second, if you're trying to mimic someone else's performance, you won't come across as true to yourself. Just as Van Gogh would never have reached his iconic status by copying Michelangelo's painting style, you and your audience will both feel strange if you copy another speaker.

Public speaking is an *art* rather than a science, because it is a creative process where a right or wrong answer only exists in terms of what's right or wrong for you. Still, Van Gogh had to learn certain techniques of colour use, brush strokes and composition so that his unique style worked. In this book I'll show you six qualities that brilliant speakers possess and the techniques for how to achieve them. I'll include some suggestions, tips and exercises to improve your public speaking, but the emphasis is always on you to develop your own style.

Public speaking secret 3: You already have everything you need to be a brilliant speaker

When it comes down to it, there's absolutely no difference between you and Martin Luther King Jr. Whilst you may not have his audience, or his moment in history, there's no reason why you shouldn't be as good as him at public speaking – or better. What I mean by this is that you naturally possess the six public speaking skills I will focus on in this book, even if you currently aren't able to use them in public speaking situations. With an injection of technique and some practice from you, you will learn that there is nothing stopping you from being a brilliant speaker.

The Public Speaking House

Each of these six public speaking qualities form the *Public Speaking House*, a model to help you grow as a speaker. Develop just a few of these qualities and your confidence and performance will dramatically improve. Master all six qualities and you will become a powerful, inspiring speaker.

The Public Speaking House has three pillars, which relate to the content of your speaking, and three layers, which relate to you as a speaker. Each of these will form a part in this book.

The Public Speaking House

The three pillars of content

Empathy: Public speakers often design their talk based on what they want to say, rather than what the audience want to hear. The best speakers know their audience intimately and shape what they say around this insight. The Empathy pillar shows you how to improve your public speaking by focusing on the needs of your audience, forgetting about your own nerves in the process.

Freshness: In a world of information overload, doing something different is critical for your success as a speaker. Freshness is thinking creatively to provide a memorable experience for your audience. Forget about 'death by PowerPoint' and learn to create innovative and exciting public speaking.

Balance: Balance in public speaking comes from the shape and structure of your material. Just like many of the greatest plays and movies, great public speaking has a powerful structure that gives the audience the right information at the right time.

The three layers of you, the speaker

Awareness: This is the foundation for all personal development and is particularly relevant in public speaking where we enter the 'twilight zone' and lose control of our actions. Only by becoming totally aware of how you are thinking, what you are saying and what you are doing as you speak can you start to acquire choice in how to behave.

Fearlessness: This is the state where you are able to do anything necessary to benefit your audience and your message. Fearlessness is about learning where the edges of your comfort zone lie and bravely stepping beyond them.

Authenticity: Each of the first five skills will make you an effective speaker. But if you want to be a truly brilliant speaker – one who can inspire or influence – you'll need to speak from the heart in a way that's authentic to you. Authenticity is about discovering your message as a speaker and being able to express it.

How to use this book

ANY AUDIENCE, ANY SITUATION: Whilst this book is designed to be read as a complete work, you may wish to focus on specific sections if you have a particular speaking assignment coming up:

Occasional speeches such as weddings

- Get a solid plan together quickly with the Content Pie – p.167.
- Flawless Memory techniques – p.179.
- Get over those nerves with a confidence visualisation – p.207.

Running an educational workshop

- Design your workshop with your audience in mind – p.63.
- Spice it up with innovative interactive techniques – p.133.
- Learn how to handle any audience type – p.89.

Delivering an informative speech

- Become aware of what your body and voice are doing whilst you're on stage – Chapter 2.
- Razzle dazzle your audience with memorable visual aids – p.121.
- Learn what your comfort zone is and how to step beyond it – pp.192 & 205.

Giving an after-dinner or motivational speech

- Conjure inspiration through the words you use – p.113.
- Build the intensity of your speech to a moving crescendo – p.158.
- Balance your internal state so you powerfully influence your audience – p.230.

WHATEVER YOUR LEVEL: Whether you're a public speaking rookie, or maestro, you can make improvements in the way you speak in public. I aim to give titbits that will encourage and inspire beginners and give the old hands new ideas to play with. What I need from you is your openness to trust the methods and try out something different from each chapter.

Watch out for the 'What if...' tips from a selection of experts – psychologists, top public speakers and voice coaches – who have kindly shared their experiences and insights on some of the most common worries people have about public speaking.

LEARNING BY DOING: learning is a two-way process, which is where personal development books often fail in comparison with training programmes. If you want to improve at public speaking, it's not enough just to read this book and *know* how to speak in public. *You can't learn French without ordering a croissant or two.* To become a competent, good or inspiring public speaker, you'll need to get stuck in with the workout tasks at the end of chapters. If you need more help, my company Ginger Training & Coaching is ready to help you. Head over to my website, www.gingerpublicspeaking.com, where there are bundles more tools, resources and opportunities to get involved with public speaking practice. If you enjoy the illustrations in this book, you'll love what you see 'over there'!

Look out for the workouts at the end of each part

BEING AUTHENTIC: Because I encourage speakers to speak from the heart and unleash their authenticity on their audience, I have tried to be as authentic as possible in presenting facts about public speaking throughout these pages. The science behind this book is grounded in scholarly studies from neuroscience, educational psychology and behavioural psychology.

Many personal development books use vague studies as their backbone, which makes me feel uncomfortable. These are often eye-catching headlines, which lack any foundation in reality. For example, the most common public speaking 'fact' I hear is a survey of fears in which public speaking came top, with death at a lowly seventh place. Whilst this was reported in 1973 by one survey,[1] this information has never been verified by scholarly sources.

However, although there's no scientific evidence I know of to demonstrate that public speaking is really the world's biggest fear, it's a real challenge for many people to whom I speak. There is a wealth of information around public speaking fear that we'll look at later.

A GOOD RESTAURANT NEEDS A SECOND VISIT: Imagine you're looking at the menu at a fine restaurant. You can't order everything at once, so you'll need to come back a number of times to taste each of the dishes. In the same way, you won't take and put into practice everything from this book on the first read. I encourage you to pick ingredients from each chapter to enrich your public speaking palette, little by little. Record these in the Ingredients List on page 241. And, just as you wouldn't order the pecan pie if you have a nut allergy, you may not use all of the tools provided either. Develop public speaking practices that feel authentic to you – that's how you'll be confident in what you're doing.

WE LEARN BEST WHEN WE'RE HAVING FUN: As neuroscience has started to show, people learn best when they feel good. Information associated with positive emotion is stored in a part of the brain called the hippocampus, which later transfers information into the long-term memory. Conversely, negative emotions such as boredom are statistically shown to lead to poorer recall of information. This is a very adult excuse for using doodles, lively examples and entertaining analogies throughout – I hope you have fun and learn whilst reading this book.

---

[1] Bruskin Associates, 'What are Americans Afraid Of?', *The Bruskin Report*, 1973, p.53. This survey isn't publicly accessible, but was reported in a *Sunday Times* article entitled, 'What People Usually Fear', 7 October 1973, p.9.

Chapter

It starts with authenticity

Let's begin at our destination by taking a quick look at what it is to be an authentic speaker. This is the roof on the Public Speaking House – the place we're trying to get to, after all of the nerves and doubts have been overcome. Authenticity is, by nature, already a part of you, so it's both a destination and a place to start.

We'll return to authenticity at the end of the book, but before we launch into the other five parts of the Public Speaking House, it's useful to keep authenticity in mind.

Brilliant public speaking comes from the heart

I've often heard the concern from aspiring public speakers that standing up in front of an audience to speak can feel fake. When we see motivational speakers, politicians and salespeople using public speaking techniques to manipulate, exaggerate, twist and even falsify information, it's easy to see why.

I strongly believe, as do so many of today's top professional speakers, that great public speaking starts with talking from the heart. Much more than good technique and a solid structure, talking from the heart is appealing and memorable because the audience connects with the speaker on an emotional level. Smart audiences can smell a 'WIFFY' speaker a mile off – a speaker who is Waffly, Inauthentic or False. Audiences are turning away from the bright lights of rhetoric and impossible promises towards humble, genuine and emotional public speaking experiences. Indeed, we've always gravitated towards the *real* speakers from Gandhi to Jamie Oliver.

And it's not just speakers with a cause – every day in business you see authentic speakers winning over their audience, from the big names like Richard Branson and Steve Jobs, through to the team leader in a meeting room.

What is perfect authenticity?

The authentic you is the real you, who's always with you wherever you go. But it's not always easy to be completely authentic when speaking in public. What we're interested in here is your ability to *express* your authenticity to an audience. To speak from the heart. And only you know for sure when you're being authentic, although others will sense it. Perfect authenticity is:

- A sense of certainty that's independent of anyone else.
- The feeling of acceptance towards your strengths and limitations.
- The knowledge that a course of action is right, even if it's not easy.

- A warm feeling of relief – that what you just said was deeply true for you.
- The feeling of power – that you can say whatever is needed.

Setting your compass

So, let's look at the first part of developing authenticity – 'setting your compass' as a speaker.

Your 'compass' is your internal sense of purpose. It's the reason why you would stand up in front of a group of people and speak. If your compass is swinging from one direction to another, you'll be unsure of why you'd put yourself through it. With a wobbly compass, public speaking can be something terrifying, frustrating or embarrassing. But if you see a good reason for speaking, if your compass is pointing north, you will be more capable of expressing yourself, because you know 'what's in it' for you.

Consider what's important to you about public speaking. What are you willing to battle through your fears and doubts to achieve? Perhaps it's your urge to get across an important message, perhaps it's to learn and grow as a person, or perhaps it's to benefit your audience in some way. It's unlikely to be 'because my boss told me to'.

If you find what's really important to you, any fear you feel will seem a small price to pay. Find your purpose and you find your authentic reason for speaking.

To set your compass, ask yourself two sets of questions:

1. What's important about speaking for me as a person?

Ask yourself:

- What is important to me about public speaking?
- What opportunities and possibilities does it deliver to me?
- What excites me about speaking?

These questions will lead you to your personal purpose for speaking, which is one side of your authentic expression.

I would never have become a public speaker unless I understood my personal purpose – I was simply too scared of it. The only reason I faced my fear of public speaking was because I realised my dream job was more important to me. Knowing what I wanted, I was able to stand up and authentically say, 'This is who I am and what I have to offer. I want the job and I know I can do it.'

2. What's important about my message?

If you struggle to speak for the sake of your own development, why not focus on all of the people you could benefit through expressing your message? Dig deep into your topic and ask yourself:

- What is my message? What effect am I *really* trying to have by speaking?
- What is important about my message to the wider world?
- What value does it bring to my audience?

If you're a campaigner or inspirational speaker, your purpose may be very obvious. But what if you're just delivering a 'mundane' message, or don't quite know what you stand for? Every speaker, whatever the topic, has the opportunity to link their words with something deeper or more inspiring. An accountant might speak because she's helping people closer to their dream lifestyle. A consultant might speak because he lives for the spark of excitement on his clients' faces. You just have to look deeper: what's *important* about your weekly team meeting? What was the original purpose behind this lecture?

Ask yourself:

- What's the biggest possible impact my message could have on the world?
- What would happen if nobody ever heard my message?

The answers to these questions are the source of your passion for your subject – and your reason to stand up and be heard.

Keep your authentic reasons for speaking in mind as we progress through the next chapters.

Part

1

Every speaker has a mouth:
An arrangement rather neat.
Sometimes it's filled with wisdom.
Sometimes it's filled with feet.

Robert Orben

As he clicked through to his 'Thank You' slide, Edgar Mumble looked up at his bored audience. 'Phew, it's over,' he thought with relief. 'That was much longer than I imagined.'

'Erm . . . any questions?' he muttered to the first row, scratching at a red patch on his neck. His offer was met with silence. Edgar collected his books and scuttled out of the room to a thin ripple of applause.

'That went well,' he said to himself, 'I'll do the same presentation again next year.'

Awareness

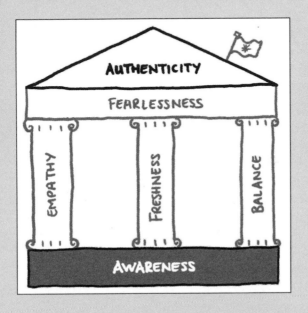

The first step to public speaking mastery is to become aware of precisely what you're doing when you speak. If you are able to master the basics and develop your strengths, you will fill your audience with the confidence that you are a speaker who can be relied on. If your audience have this confidence in you, they will focus on the bit you want them to focus on, your message, rather than any quirks of your public speaking skills.

Without awareness, you simply don't know whether you're wowing or boring your audience.

What is perfect awareness?

Awareness is the conscious space for choice. With awareness you begin to distance yourself from what you're doing, so you can start to choose which bits of your performance function well and which don't. From there you can begin to change, to give the audience greater openness to your message.

Perfect awareness means:

- Being conscious of what you're saying and how you're saying it, as you're saying it.
- Being in control of your body and speech, so that they don't detract from what you're saying.
- Using your body and speech to enhance your public speaking message.

How do you develop awareness?

To gain awareness, first of all you need the curiosity to improve, wherever your starting point. I guess that's why you've picked up this book. Without that motivation, you'll stay like our Edgar Mumble – more satisfied with your performance than your audience is.

Once you've got the curiosity you can start looking at specific parts of your performance to see what you currently do that you were blissfully unaware of, and how you can swap those behaviours for something more powerful.

In this part we'll look at your body and voice – the areas of your performance I call your **Speaker's Toolkit**. Through these tools you have the power to inspire, intrigue or incite your audience.

Chapter

Add the most important sites to your Favorites List (har)

Your body

Let's jump into the world of Rude Awakenings by hunting down the behaviours in your body and voice that are embarrassing. Once we've identified the parts that need improving, you'll learn how to transform them into the behaviours of the experts.

Body

We'll look at the body from the top down. For each element of your body, work to minimise the 'embarrassing' and maximise the 'expert' in your performance in a way that feels authentic to you. Add the most important ones to your Ingredients List (page 241).

Eyes

Consider how easy it is to ignore or drift off from a video, a podcast or a conference call. Even when you're watching a live webcast of a speech or presentation, it's easier to drift off than if you were in the room. At least part of this is because of the lack of eye contact between you and the speaker.

When a speaker makes eye contact with their audience, the audience feel like an exchange, a conversation, is taking place. In a conversation we expect to participate, so we listen more effectively.

Become aware of where your eyes are going as you speak. There are four possibilities that you should avoid, as follows:

Embarrassing places to find your eyes

1. **Eyes that are . . . glued to the floor or ceiling**

   Imagine you're watching a speaker who stares up at the floor or ceiling, but rarely looks at the audience. What message does that give you about their abilities? Usually it's a message that they're lacking in confidence, unsure of their material, unprepared or uninterested in the subject. A common perception is that a speaker looking up is either recalling information or making it up. Although this popular belief isn't supported by research, it hardly matters, if that's what the audience think of you. Be aware of how audiences make snap judgements based on what you do with your Speaker's Toolkit.

   As a nervous speaker, it's tempting to search the ceiling for a clue about what to say next. It's just one of the tricks the mind plays on us when we're out of our comfort zone. When I first started speaking I imagined that if I looked the audience in the eyes, they would somehow know I was feeling nervous, I was faking it and I didn't have all the answers about my topic. Making eye contact with them was like a horrible moment of realisation that I was *actually* up on stage and everyone could see me there. Or worse still, I worried that if I caught the eye of a particularly negative member of the audience, their scornful look might just turn me into dust, right there on stage. *It could happen.*

   Having tested it for years, I can say with confidence that this won't happen. But what I mean to do is to alert you to your own patterns of thinking about your performance. If you avoid eye contact, then why is that? What's the worst that could happen if you connect to your audience?

   You'll realise that eye contact with the audience actually feels great. It's your way to see that people understand what you're saying (more on this when we look at empathy) and the more you make that connection, the more confident you'll feel about what you are saying.

> **Expert eye contact tip 1:** Once you've brought your eyes down from the ceiling, stay in the zone of the audience's upper bodies. If you need space to think, continue to look towards your audience, but unfocus your eyes.

> **Expert eye contact tip 2:** If you look in-between someone's eyes, to them it will seem like you're looking them straight in the eyes. It's fine to do this if you really feel nervous, but I prefer that genuine connection where you see what the other person is thinking.

2. Eyes that are . . . hanging on to a lifeline

The next eye contact mistake is to find one or two people in the audience who seem to be friendly – a familiar face, or someone (anyone!) who's smiling at you – and cling to them. These are 'lifelines', to whom inexperienced speakers often give too much attention. Think about how the rest of the audience feels if you're only focused on one person.

If you were in a three-way conversation and only making eye contact with one person, the third would quickly walk away. An audience don't always have the same freedom, but instead of walking away physically, they may start to wander off mentally from what you're saying, simply because it feels like you're not saying it to them.

> **Expert eye contact tip 3:** Ensure you make eye contact with everyone in your room, front to back, left to right. This is sometimes tricky if people are slightly behind you, but don't neglect them. If you're in a small group, you'll be looking to give every person two to three seconds of eye contact at a time. That's long enough to make each person feel spoken to, but not long enough to make them uncomfortable.

▶

If you're in a larger group, focus on clusters of people who seem to 'have a rapport' with each other. Look for groups who mirror or match each other's body language and treat them as you would an individual person, spending two to three seconds on each cluster. This doesn't need to be too scientific, you can go with your feeling on where different groups of audience members are collecting.

3. Eyes that are . . . burrowed into your notes

The third no-no of eye contact is to spend too much time delving into your notes when you could be looking at your audience. This can happen when you don't feel confident in your material, or when it's precise or complex information. Like Edgar Mumble at the beginning of this chapter, burrowing is a curse that often befalls those who use a lectern for their speech. A lectern, aside from being a barrier between yourself and the audience, offers a hiding place for potentially limitless notes. The more notes you have, the more confusing they will be when you're speaking and so the more you will tend to rely on speaking word by word from the notes. As this happens, your eye contact with the audience reduces to a quick glance here and there.

When a speaker is talking *at* their audience, rather than to or with them, the audience will switch off. And if your audience have switched off, you might as well be standing in an empty room talking to yourself.

> **Expert eye contact tip 4:** As you're preparing your speech or talk, condense your important messages into a one-page format that you can glance at and know where to go to next. We'll look at structuring what you say in more detail in Chapter 8.

> **Expert eye contact tip 5:** Encourage eye contact by leaving your lectern, especially if you want to deliver a message that's dynamic, engaging or humorous. You can either leave your notes on the lectern to return to (you don't need your notes as much as you think), or make small, palm-sized note cards to glance at occasionally.

Hands

Moving down the body, we find two wonderful implements in our Speaker's Toolkit – our hands. Like a hammer, these are tools that can be used with precision and effect, or with disastrous consequences.

Most rookie public speakers have a fiddle or fidget. Whilst that's no problem in small doses, an untamed fidget can pull the attention of the audience away from what you're saying and give them the perception that you're not confident. This will make them close off to your message and start to doubt you.

If the audience don't trust you, you'll pick up subtle (and sometimes unsubtle) clues of impatience, ranging from folded arms, to interrupting, to rude questions. Who would think this could all come from a simple fidget? Yet everything you do whilst public speaking is sending signals to your audience about how they should behave.

Bring your fiddles and fidgets under control by getting feedback about them. Once you're aware of what you're doing, you can gradually take control.

> ## What if . . . I lose control of my body parts when I speak?
>
> *Expert tip: Dr Graeme Codrington*
>
> Dr Graeme Codrington is a future trends specialist who was recently voted 'Speaker of the Year' by the Academy for Chief Executives. He regularly speaks to audiences of 20 to 6,000 people. Graeme says that losing control of a part of your body when you're speaking is actually a good sign:
>
> 'Understand that everyone gets nervous when they care about their public speaking. An out-of-control body part is nothing more than a sign that your body is experiencing nerves. Physically what is happening is that your brain is requesting more oxygen from your system. Your system starves another part of your body of that oxygen and diverts it to the brain. This helps you be sharper and speak better, but it leaves you with the symptoms of nerves that you feel.
>
> 'It shows that you care about your message, so it's not something to worry about. Once you notice what's going on, you can acknowledge, accept and overcome it. I'm lucky that I don't have flailing arms or wobbly knees, it's my stomach that tells me I'm nervous, so only I know that. I overcome my nerves by not eating before I go on stage. If your knees knock, stand behind a lectern at the beginning – find a solution that works for you.
>
> 'The worst thing is when people don't know they're nervous, because they will do something weird without knowing it. I once watched a speaker give his whole presentation with his finger in his ear. It was only after he saw himself back on video that he realised he was doing it.'

When you've cured your fiddles and fidgets, the other possible downfall is making the audience feel like they've landed in Italy. Constant hand waving as you desperately try to express yourself can distract the audience or give them the wrong message about you.

So, how do you bring your gestures under control? First, by being aware of some of the possible mistakes you could make and then, by replacing those Grim Gestures with Gorgeous Gestures. Here are the top eight of each.

Eight Grim Gestures

8. **Clicky-Clicky:** Ever been in a talk where the speaker, oblivious to their own actions, has spent five minutes or more clicky-clicking on their biro? If you've experienced that, you'll notice your attention is pulled there and the speaker's words blur into the background. Why would a speaker need a biro anyway? If you're at risk of clicking, just put the pen down.

7. **The Jab:** Too much pointing is rarely received well by an audience. Whether it's pointing directly at people, or jabbing into your hand, it comes across as aggressive or accusatory and can make your audience feel attacked. Soften it up by pointing with your whole hand.

6. **The Tony Blair:** 'Education, education, education' and the accompanying hand slicing movement. Whilst this gesture is controlled and powerful, fans of the 'noughties' will notice we're in a different decade now. Audiences are looking for empathy and the Tony Blair is no longer a gesture that carries a message of authenticity. Avoid this and other gestures borrowed from public figures if you want to seem genuine.

5. **Quick, Hide!** I often see new speakers try to hide themselves due to nerves. They pull nervously on their sleeves to cover a little bit more skin. Guess what? The audience will still be able to see you anyway. Wear clothes you feel confident in and take the floor with pride.

4. **Clapping and Slapping:** Whilst a well-placed hand clap can add emphasis to your main points, overdo it and it becomes a distraction. This could be hand clapping or – often – unintended hitting of your hand against your side or knees. It's distracting. If you're hankering after applause, wait until you've finished.

3. **The Wringer:** One of the most common Grim Gestures in business, this is holding your hands together and massaging the palms with each other. Great for a masseur warming up, but to your audience you come across as tense, indecisive and possibly a touch aggressive.

2. **The Seven Minute Itch:** Of all the weird and wonderful ways adrenaline plays with our hands when we're nervous, itching and scratching must be the most distasteful. I've seen speakers almost scratch holes into their necks, arms etc. in moments of high stress. What should you do about it? First, notice what you're doing. You'll realise, if you pause for a moment, that there's a repetitive action going on and it's beginning to hurt! Then, relax your hands. Breathe some oxygen into them and place your hands – calmly – somewhere they can do no harm.

1. **Fly Swatting:** And finally, holding the Number 1 spot is the classic Fly Swatting gesture. There is no gesture more grim than general arm waving that goes on and on and on, no matter what the speaker is saying. The key here is power. If your gestures are weak, your authority as a speaker will be weak and thus the message you're trying to get across will be weakened (whether it's a sales pitch, a training programme or a wedding speech, we all have a message). Concentrate on making your gestures definite, and appropriate to your message, rather than too general.

Once you've tamed your Grim Gestures, it's good to have a safe space you can return your hands to, no matter what. The basic minimum to replace them with is a neutral point.

The Neutral Point: Draw your hands up to your middle and keep them springy and ready for action. Your hands should be in a comfortable, very loose fist. From here, you're ready for anything and you can also sneak some notes into one hand if you like. This is a much more powerful neutral point than holding your arms down by your legs (lacking in energy), in your pockets (lazy looking) or with your arms folded (which appears passive or closed). Some people like to hold their hands together in this Neutral Point. This also works, as long as you keep your hands still.

Return to your neutral point whenever your hands aren't doing anything else. Don't worry if it feels funny to start with. This gesture is designed to look normal to the audience, so they won't notice – and in a short while it will feel natural to you too.

Eight Gorgeous Gestures

Now onto the stuff of the experts. Here are eight ways to use gestures to create more impact.

8. **Finger Counting:** As simple as it gets. If you have three points to make in your talk, signpost those three points for your audience with a one, two and three on your fingers. This helps them follow your structure and remember what you said. Make sure that your fingers are held out solidly and at shoulder level, rather than waving them around.

9. The Bottom Line: If you're delivering a firm message and want to seem authoritative without being aggressive, the Bottom Line is a useful gesture. It's a waist-height slow sweep outwards from arms crossed over like an 'x' to arms spread out. Your palms are face down and it looks a little like you're smoothing out a sheet. This gesture says, 'That's my final decision' or 'No further discussion needed.' It is pacifying, yet assertive.

6. **Sound Effects:** Your hands are more than just pointing pieces. If you want to make impact at a key moment in your speech, try a clap of the hands or a click of the fingers. Not so many speakers do this, so it brings a new layer of drama and energy to your performance. But be careful not to over-use sound effects. You want them to slip under the radar of your audience so that they emphasise your message, but don't draw attention away from it.

Here's how it might work:

'No matter how much I thought about it, I couldn't work out how to convince him I'm right. And then it hit me [slap of hands] – I didn't need to.'

If you are using a microphone, test out your sound effect before speaking, so you know it will work.

5. **Dealing Cards:** Often we want to create agreement with our audience and this is the perfect gesture for this effect. Dealing Cards is an open palm held upwards, with a movement as if you're throwing a card to a member of the audience. This gesture subtly gives permission for the audience to involve themselves in what you're saying – either mentally, or practically, by asking or answering questions. You can deal your cards to general sections of the audience, or to just one person if you're seeking that individual's involvement.

4. **Cherry-picking:** Here's one of my favourite gestures, which is ideal for the precise bits of your message. Bring your fore-finger and thumb together as if you were picking a cherry in front of you and gesture with those two fingers forward. This gives the effect of you plucking some very specific infor-mation out of air and will satisfy the logical minds in your audience. For example:

'There are two things I'd like to pick up on here. First, Matthew has designed and built more than 50 [cherry-pick] websites and second, that our company [cherry-pick] pro-vides the best value you'll find.'

The second cherry-pick shows how you can use inferred pre-cision in your gestures to influence your audience. In this case the inference is that 'our company' has been cherry-picked especially for the audience.

5. **Powerful Fist Clench:** If you're looking for an emotional lift, a clenched fist can work for a variety of powerful messages, like 'Yes, we did it,' 'Let's be strong', or 'This is going to work'. Using the fist clench is a bold move, but put it into the key moment in your speech and the audience will feel its power. Whilst this would typically be considered a masculine gesture, it can be powerful for a woman to use it, as a contrast to a feminine style.

2. **Space Putty:** Imagine you had all the possible visual aids you need, without ever needing a projector, flipchart or broom cupboard. The good news is that you have – in your hands. Great speakers I've seen mould and shape their space to create props for themselves. If you're telling a story about a kitten, why not open you palm and refer to the kitten sitting right there?

   My favourite use of Space Putty is to put different concepts or different parts of a speech into different parts of my performance space. Let me explain. If I gesture up-right as I refer to the Blue Penguin, that's where the Blue Penguin will sit in the minds of the audience. If I gesture down-left to the Giant Bumblebee, that's where the Giant Bumblebee will live. I can then come back later and pick up, examine or play with my Space Putty bumblebee or penguin. This helps your audience to engage their imagination and visualise your points more clearly. Be creative.

3. **Iconic Gestures:** Best of all, develop a unique way to emphasise your message through gestures. An Iconic Gesture is a gesture you return to time and again in your speech whenever your main message shows up. Choose the most important moments in what you're saying – the bits you'd like your audience to remember – and find gestures that fit. Don't be afraid to be bold. An unusual gesture will stick in the minds of your audience more effectively.

   Churchill's 'V' for Victory is one of the most famous Iconic Gestures. The 'V' was powerful not only because Churchill used it frequently, but because it reinforced his message – 'I will lead us to victory'.

Here's how you might use an Iconic Gesture:

Imagine a speaker's assignment to MC the 'Young Stars' awards ceremony. He may choose an Iconic Gesture that's like a starburst – from a closed fist to an open hand, fingers spreading out like a starburst. He could use it throughout the evening at key moments when he's talking about the admirable qualities of the award winners.

Each time a starburst-like gesture is made by this speaker, he will reinforce the theme of the evening. A starburst reflects the energy and sparkle of the award recipients and also mirrors the name of the awards. Therefore repeating this gesture will strengthen the speaker's key messages.

Notice that each of these 'expert' gestures could be embarrassing if they clash with your character, your level of confidence in delivering them, or your message. Work out which ones feel authentic to you and your message and only use those you feel comfortable with.

To work on your gestures more, study other public speakers as you watch them in action. Who has power as a speaker? Who fails to keep your attention? How do their gestures contribute to this?

Key rules for Gorgeous Gestures

- Choose gestures that fit with your style.
- Use gestures to highlight key parts of your message.
- Keep mixing up the texture of your gestures. Don't use the same gesture too frequently.
- Deliver gestures powerfully and with no flappy fuss.
- Take note of the format of your speech when deciding your gestures. Will you have a microphone? Will you be filmed? How big is your audience? These are all factors that will affect how large your gestures need to be and in which part of your body space.

Posture

Next stop on our trip around the body is your posture, or the way you hold your body.

Think back to your school days. You're in class waiting for your regular teacher to arrive and the door swings open. In shuffles a weather-beaten figure, hunched over with a heavy bag. Her shoulders are pinched forwards and her head down. This is your substitute teacher for the day. She scurries to her desk and sorts out her papers, all of her limbs pointing inwards slightly.

'Right children . . .', she says, 'let's turn to page 52.'

How do you think that day's going to go?

Like it or not, the way you hold yourself makes an immediate impression on your audience. So how do you make sure you kick off on the right foot, whilst avoiding being perceived as arrogant?

1. Be aware of how you're holding yourself

Look at yourself in a mirror before you carry out your speaking assignment. Is your body language positive and open, or defensive?

You will look most confident with a neutral, open posture with the following characteristics:

- Shoulders back, head balanced comfortably on your shoulders;
- Your chest filled with air and positioned slightly upwards (too much and you'll look like a robin);
- Feet positioned shoulder-width apart;
- Nicely balanced on both legs equally, with your knees loose to bend slightly.

As research confirms, open postures are associated with feelings of power. If you have a confident posture, the audience will see you as more powerful and you will feel more powerful as a speaker.

Having open posture in turn creates a virtuous circle with breathing. It allows more oxygen to enter your lungs, which then helps you to think more clearly and give a more confident performance.

What if . . . I'm worried about my appearance on stage?

Expert tip: Lesley Everett

Personal Branding expert and author of *Walking Tall*, Lesley Everett advises public speakers on how to give the right impression through what they wear. She says:

'As with your posture, your clothing speaks volumes about you and your message, so don't underestimate its importance. Your clothing is part of the brand that your audience will subconsciously absorb as you speak. If your clothing doesn't represent your message, you will dilute your impact.

'If you want to look confident "on stage", begin by defining the message you want to leave your audience with. Is it a serious message? Then dress accordingly. Do you want to emphasise your fun personality? Choose a tie, shoes, or accessory that's quirky. To stand out as a speaker, pay attention to the details. Even a small stain will be noticed and scrutinised by someone in the audience. Always get someone to check your "rear" for the bits you can't see. If you're representing a company, try mirroring key elements of the brand in what you're wearing. My company, Walking TALL, has a giraffe as a logo, so I sometimes reflect that by wearing touches of yellow, or animal print.

'The most important thing is how your outfit makes you feel. It has a huge impact on a speaker to look and feel good on stage, so dress in a way that's both authentic and powerful for you and it will support your confidence. Overall, if your outfit "fits" it will not be a distraction and your audience will be focused on you and what you have to say.'

---

2. Be aware of your attitude

If, for whatever reason, you don't want to do your speech or talk, your body will show that by trying to hide from all the people looking at you. This can be as obvious as trying to hide in the corner of your stage, or as subtle as hunching your shoulders together. The root cause of your posture is your attitude towards yourself and your ability to speak in public. Try to notice the following in yourself:

● How do I feel about this speech or talk?
● Do I really believe I can do a good job?
● How does that affect my body?
● Where does it make me tense or tight?

By becoming aware of tension in your body, you're taking one step towards being able to do something about it. Once you're aware, you can take a few moments before you start speaking to consciously relax and open out those parts of your body.

Your posture will improve as soon as you take ownership of your stage. Be proud of yourself – see it as a privilege to be asked to speak in any situation. After all, if you've been asked to talk, you must have been chosen for a reason. Perhaps it's for your character, your connection to the topic in question, or the knowledge you have. Either way, a confident, relaxed attitude will transfer into a confident, relaxed posture.

Legs

Our final stop in the body are the legs. All sorts of funny things happen to the body when we're pumped with adrenaline and feel under pressure. Be aware. Here are some of the most common embarrassing things that can happen to your legs.

Jelly legs

The very first time I spoke in public, my legs were quivering. I remember thinking, 'How can I speak when I can't even stand?' It's easy to panic if that happens, because it feels like your very foundations may fall out from under you. The good news is that this feeling passes quickly if you let it. Even better news is that your audience won't be able to see a quiver here and there, so put it out of your mind.

Michael Jackson feet

So your legs haven't collapsed yet, congratulations. Now the next challenge rears its head. If, like the Jackson 5, you just *can't control your feet*, this is for you. Excessive shuffling about from one foot to the other makes you seem nervy and uncertain. Frankly, sometimes it looks more like you have to go to the toilet than you're speaking in public.

As a basic minimum, drop your Michael Jackson moonwalk and allow your feet (both of them) to settle flat on the floor. Remember the open position and place your feet shoulder-width apart and allow yourself to feel comfortable and balanced. If you can do nothing else, no movement is better than too much movement. Planting yourself to the spot will seem a touch static, especially if you're delivering a longer talk, or standing on a big stage, but it's a minimum that will put your audience at ease.

Is that a spider running up my leg?

One of the funny tricks adrenaline plays on us is to make us feel uncomfortable or itchy in places of which we'd never otherwise be conscious. You may find your legs crossing over to subconsciously protect yourself from the audience, or rubbing against each other to kill an imaginary spider. Whether or not there *is* a spider running up your leg, crossing your legs doesn't show you in your best light. Because you're not stable in your body, your audience will pick up on your message as being less reliable than if you are centred. Crossing your legs indicates discomfort and inexperience. And more than that, if you're not planted firmly on the ground you'll *feel* more uncomfortable and off balance. Gently bring your legs back to that static spot, shoulder-width apart.

The Rocking Horse

I once saw a business leader at a networking event for 300 people spend 20 minutes speaking with one foot in front of the other, rocking gently backwards and forward. By the end of his presentation I felt a little seasick and couldn't remember a word he said.

Any repetitive movement performed without awareness has the potential to steal your show and the Rocking Horse is one of the most common. This movement points to uncertainty, that you're not completely committed to what you're saying. Commit to your movements and you'll signal commitment to your message.

Courtside at Wimbledon

Once you feel comfortable on your feet, you may wish to start integrating movement into your performance. This has lots of benefits. You can influence a larger room, you appear more dynamic and if done correctly, it can build on your message.

But, as with any of the tips in the Speaker's Toolkit, if you use movement too much it will disturb your audience. If the audience have to move their heads back and forth to follow you they will start to feel like they're watching a tennis match. If you see lots of neck craning going on, you're making your audience work too hard. If they've stopped looking at you altogether, you've worn them out.

Likewise, if you're talking around a table, movement is not needed. In these situations if you move, you'll be walking behind people's backs, which either forces them to bend at unusual angles, or gives the audience the impression of being stalked.

Unless your intention is to come across as slightly predatory, avoid wandering around behind chairs.

How to use movement with conviction

So if those are movements to avoid, how do the experts use movement to dazzle their audience? Here are some of the best ways to use your available space in a creative and purposeful manner:

Authority versus space: To put authority behind a point, move slightly towards your audience. To encourage them to think, step away a touch, putting more space between you and them.

Different sides of the stage for contrasting points: If you have a structure that is comparing two sides of an argument (see Chapter 8 for more on structure), you could set up one side of your room for option A and the other side for option B. Every time you mention a point for option A, walk to that side of the room and deliver that point standing still. To speak about option B, move to that side of the room. To toss up between the two, stand in the middle, pick a winner and head to the winning side of the room to deliver a conclusion. Get this right and you'll look like a pro.

Time-lining your stage: In Western culture, past to future generally runs from left to right. In the minds of your audience, therefore, *their* left is a good place to stand when you're talking about the past and as you move forwards in time, you can move towards their right. The same is true when you're presenting the old (bad) versus the new (good). The right side of the stage holds a subconscious positive position in the minds of the audience. Don't forget that this is the opposite from what you'll experience as the speaker.

The Crab Walk: It's not a good idea to turn your back on part of the audience when you're moving about the stage. Seeing a speaker's back can make audience members feel shunned. Get round this by moving like a crab. This means that your body always faces forwards, but you cross one leg in front of the other as you walk. Keep your steps wide and slow to make sure you keep your balance.

Chapter

3

Your voice

Now our awareness turns to the second major tool in your Speaker's Toolkit – your voice. There are five tools of your voice to master, each of which forms one letter of the 'VOICE' model.

With each of the five, I'll help you gain awareness of embarrassing mistakes to avoid and show you how to impress like an expert.

 O I C E

V is for – Volume

Volume is one of those 'must get right' factors in a speech. At a basic minimum, your audience will never be able to take in your message if they can't hear you speak.

Can you hear me at the back?

Your first consideration is your own voice. Are you softly spoken or a Brian Blessed boomer? If you have a booming voice you're in luck. Your audience will have no trouble hearing you. Just be careful not to blow your audience away, especially if you're using a microphone (more on this below).

Here's how to get your volume just right:

1. The traditional 'Can you hear me at the back?' is a good question to ask if you have no other way of checking in on your volume. However, this approach has a couple of problems. First, it's frustrating for the audience if there is a long line of

speakers, each of whom asks 'Can you hear me at the back?' before they start. Although it may be novel for you to utter those famous words, it's not an enticing first line. Your first words are your opportunity to open with either a *bang* or a *flop*, so use them wisely. Whenever possible, do your sound check before people enter the room, by asking a colleague or fellow speaker to stand at the back and check they can hear. Remember, when the room is full, some of your volume will be dulled by the bodies, so you'll need to project your voice more.

Second, even if people can hear you at the back to begin with, if your voice then becomes softer further into your talk, it's unlikely that an audience will tell you. They are much more likely to drift off as listening becomes is too much of a struggle. Instead, get yourself an 'anchor' at the back of the room to let you know if you're too quiet. Agree a gesture for them to make to you if you need to speak up. I use a pushing upwards gesture with my anchor.

2. Learn to project your voice. Most people are able to speak up more than they think with a little practice, but it sometimes takes seeing a specialist voice coach to help them get there. Whilst this is a specialist subject in itself, here are a few quick things you can do to increase projection. Start with developing the confidence to make yourself feel bigger within the room (see p. 205 for tips on building confidence). Notice that I said 'bigger' rather than 'louder'. Think of volume as you and your message filling the room, rather than shouting, which isn't appealing to any audience.

Practice relaxation of the vocal chords by humming and yawning to stretch the muscles. Now, holding your confidence inside you, push air from your stomach upwards and speak from there, rather than from your throat. It can help to imagine you're aiming your words at a target on the back of the room.

3. If your audience size is heading into the 50+ territory, or if there are sound distractions nearby, you'll want to consider using a microphone. It can be a scary prospect to hear your own voice bouncing back at you, but if this means your audi-

ence can definitely hear you, then go for it. If there's even the slightest strain on your audience's ears, you'll lose some of them, so it's worth it.

On the mic

Before you use a mic, check the following:

● The mic must be charged enough to last for your whole talk (check with the sound person).

● You know where the on/off switch is.

● You've found the best distance between the mic and your mouth.

● You know the range of the mic and where you should stand to avoid those horrible feedback screeches.

Turning it up

Although volume is one of the most basic tools in the Speaker's Toolkit, it is also an advanced tool for injecting power into your public speaking.

You've probably experienced that moment when you're in a crowded room, trying to tell your conversation partner something secret. At that moment the whole room suddenly stops talking. People instinctively find fascination in information that should be secret. You can use this human tendency to your advantage in your public speaking.

Here's how it works. If you're telling a story, or giving some information you want to emphasise, just drop your volume slightly. The audience should still be able to hear you, but you've hushed your volume to the level of a secret. Suddenly any audience members who were drifting off have their curiosity triggered, and they're back with you. Then hit home a key message at a louder than normal volume, for example:

Did you know [lower volume] we've done outstandingly well this year? We've brought in [now increase volume] double the total donations of the past two years combined.

If you have the confidence to alter volume, you'll really start to create an emotional show for your audience.

O is for ... Gaps

O is for gaps, not because of the letter 'O', but because of what's inside the 'O' – a gap! Tenuous, possibly, but memorable. As we'll see in the Freshness chapters, information that is unusual but relevant to the subject matter helps memory.

Use of gaps is one of the biggest differentiators between rookie speakers and experts. Rookies often talk quickly to get off stage, whereas experts use considered and powerful pacing. If you want to impress an audience, few techniques are more powerful than learning to 'mind the gap'. There are two types of gap you need to be aware of: gaps between words and gaps between sections of content.

1. Gaps between words

Haveyouevercomeacrossanervousspeakerwhotalkssoquicklythatalloftheir wordsseemtomergeintooneandyoucan'tunderstandanythingthey'resaying?

Time can play funny tricks on us when we're public speaking. As a result, it's easy to speak too fast without noticing. When you have so much to worry about, from your opening lines, to your gestures, to remembering your thank yous, it can be easy to forget one of the basics – to speak at a speed that your audience can follow.

There are three different 'states', or patterns of behaviour and emotion, that can cause you to speak too fast for your audience.

Butterfly State

You're nervous, flustered and anxious. You can't wait to get through your speech. Adrenaline is pulsing through your body and your speech comes out as a jumble of words at breakneck speed.

If this happens to you then ask yourself why the situation is making you nervous. Is there someone particular in the audience you see as intimidating? What's riding on the occasion? What are you telling yourself will happen if you mess up?

There's more about overcoming nerves later (see p. 205), but to overcome the Butterfly State you'll first need awareness that you're in it. Once you've recognised it, calm yourself down by having a sip of water and resolving to speak slower, or focus on your breath to slow down your heart rate.

You may need to speak so slowly that to you it feels ridiculous. But so long as you're not speaking slowly enough to put your audience to sleep, slower speaking will usually come across as more authoritative. Your apparent calmness will help the audience to have trust in you.

Tigger State

It's also possible that too much enthusiasm for a topic will leave your audience chasing your words. This can easily happen during toasts, or when explaining something you're particularly excited about. Rather than pacing yourself, the temptation is to get everything out all at once. This is counterproductive, because the information will have to be repeated if it's not understood the first time.

To help you out of the Tigger State, remember these insights:

1. Words take longer to travel across a room than across a coffee table. What would be understood in a lively conversation is likely to be too fast for an audience.

2. Conversations have a natural rhythm of 'you speak, I speak', so there is always time for each party to absorb information. This isn't the case with a speech or presentation, where there's a one-way flow of information. This means you need to slow down more than you think.

If you're looking to give an enthusiastic performance, speaking with fewer gaps between your words is not the way to do it. For different ways to add energy to your public speaking, see p. 49.

Resident Expert State

The third reason you might speak too quickly for an audience is if you fail to appreciate the difference between your level of knowledge and theirs. If information seems obvious to you – whether it's technical knowledge, or something as simple as where the fire exits are – you may be tempted to speak faster to get through the information.

To check whether you're in this state, notice how your audience are responding to you. If they can understand you fully, you'll receive eye contact and nods to affirm they are receiving your information. If you're going too slowly, you may perceive impatient fidgeting from a few members of the audience. If you're speaking too quickly, your audience may indicate that they're struggling to keep up by uncomfortable facial gestures, leaning forwards slightly or taking frantic notes.

2. Gaps between sections

Once you have your gaps between words well paced, your audience will comfortably understand your message. Research has shown that pauses help an audience recall your message at a later date.

This is one of the advanced techniques that will take you from a rookie to a maestro.

There are three different building blocks of public speaking: themes, sections and details. Each has its own degree of importance and needs slightly different use of gaps:

Themes are like acts in a play. Like most modern plays with their three acts, a good speech or presentation will have three themes. When you start a new theme, leave a substantial gap – around five seconds – to show that a major shift is happening in the speech.

Sections are like scenes in a play. A section is a substantial chunk of information that relates to the theme. A new section is best signalled by a two- to three-second pause.

Details are comparable to the lines in a play. As a new line indicates in written language, after each detail a gap is necessary. Your gap here only needs to be a second, or a fraction of a second. It should be enough for you to take a breath and allow your point to be absorbed. Emphasising to yourself that there should be even a small gap after each point will make sure you pace your public speaking well.

Making gaps authentic

Gaps can sometimes feel artificial. To avoid this feeling, try one of these expert tricks to create a gap that feels legitimate:

- Take a sip of water.
- Take a step away from the audience to check your notes. (NB, there's no need to say, 'Let me just check my notes.')
- Change your PowerPoint slide or flipchart sheet without saying anything.
- Ask your audience a question, e.g. 'Any questions from that section?'

The Powerful Pause

The ability to use gaps for dramatic effect distinguishes the average from the outstanding public speaking performance. Take a deep breath, because to pull this off you'll need the confidence to pause for longer than feels comfortable. Here's how to prepare for a powerful pause:

1. You don't want to overuse this trick, or you'll be testing your audience's intelligence and patience. So identify the one or two key messages or key moments in your talk that you want to emphasise – the moments of the highest emotion or most compelling information.

2. Shape your key moment into a sentence that's snappy and easy to remember. The shorter the better. Practise it out loud to get the feel of the sentence right.

3. Now add emphasis to this key moment. Deliver the sentence and then leave a gap. Hold it. And then hold it a little bit more. Wait for a subtle shift that will come over the audience as your point sinks in. If your key moment is well constructed or delivered it will feel like a slight 'wow' or gasp.

Hit a powerful pause and you'll transform in the eyes of the audience from hammy to Hamlet. Without gaps, a famous speech is nothing more than a collection of slightly confusing words:

'To be or not to be that's the question whether it's nobler in the mind to suffer the slings and arrows of outrageous fortune or to take arms against a sea of troubles and by opposing end them?'

But with gaps it becomes an iconic speech (wherever your Hamlet might place his pauses):

'To be, or not to be: [pause]

That [mini pause] is the question: [pause]

Whether 'tis nobler in the mind to suffer

The slings and arrows of outrageous fortune, [pause]

Or to take arms against a sea of troubles, [pause]

And by opposing end them?' [pause]

V O I C E

I is for... Intonation

Intonation is the rise and fall in voice pitch as you speak. As with all of the Speaker's Toolkit, your first task is to develop awareness of how you use intonation. Which of the following categories do you best fit into? You can find out by asking an honest friend or recording yourself speaking.

1. Robot Voice

We've all sat through a lecture or a talk where the speaker – apparently oblivious to everyone in the audience – talks with absolutely no variation in intonation. This gives the impression that even the speaker isn't interested in their material. There are few things more off-putting than a Robot Voice, but for speakers who have certain voice types, it is easy to slip into. Be particularly aware if you are male with a low voice, or if you are talking about a long and complex subject. As soon as you notice you've slipped into Robot Voice, find a way to inject passion into your next words.

What if . . . I have a naturally monotone voice?

Expert tip: Guy Ellis

Professional speaker Guy Ellis uses his voice as an important tool in engaging audiences of directors and senior managers across Europe and the Middle East. Here is his advice on intonation:

'If your voice is monotonous, you could take voice coaching. But if you find your *passion*, your voice will change automatically and a lot of your problems will go away. Even if you are the one landed presenting next year's budget, find the passion in your topic by looking for the part that fires you up. What's important about a long, boring budget? Maybe this is how your company is going to succeed next year. If success gets you passionate, use that to bring passion into your voice.

'If intonation is difficult, try varying your voice through a change in speed, quality or the number of pauses you're using. This will keep your audience on their toes and give you a chance to reflect on the effect your changes are having on the room.'

---

2. Dog Talker

At the other end of the spectrum we have speakers who use intonation that's too high or too contrasting to feel comfortable for the audience. Think about an excited conversation going on between two women with high voices (sorry ladies). If their intonation becomes too high-pitched, they may be able to communicate with each other and also dogs, but an audience will find such intonation exhausting.

3. Storyteller

Remember back to school when you gathered on the carpet for story time? What made the story so great, aside from the chance to sit on the carpet, was probably the teacher's storytelling voice. This is the state to which Robot Voices and Dog Talkers should aspire. A great storyteller will vary their intonation, along with their use of volume and gaps, to bring you inside the story. If you want your audience to feel a part of *your* story, use intonation to add sparkle and drama.

C is for . . . Clarity

How clear is your voice? As well as volume and intonation, you need to deliver your message with crystal-clear clarity.

One cause of lack of clarity could be your accent or a lack of diction. If it's your diction that is making your voice unclear try doing a few tongue twisters before you start. If you have a strong accent, be particularly careful to leave those gaps between your words and sections.

If you want to do more work on accent, see a specialist who can retrain your vocal chords, palate and tongue to help you speak more clearly.

The second cause of lack of clarity is a lack of clarity of thought or structure, which we'll tackle in Chapter 8. This section focuses on the third cause of lack of clarity: the clutter words that can sneak into speech. There are two types of clutter words, as follows.

1. The dreaded 'um'

'Um' and 'erm' are fillers which, if used frequently in public speaking, will cause you to seem unprofessional, confused or under-prepared. One or two 'ums' will go unnoticed by your audience and are natural in speaking. But without awareness, it's easy to develop a bad 'um' habit that distracts your audience, for example:

'Good morning, erm. *I wanted to welcome you,* um, *to this very special occasion,* erm, *where we'll be putting our heads together,* um, *on the topic of China's economy.'*

Think how much more powerful these words would have been if instead of 'ums' the speaker had left gaps. This can only happen if we're aware and in control of our speech.

Why do we 'um'?

Fillers are a method we use in conversations to hold space whilst we think or finish making a point. They indicate to our conversation partner that they shouldn't talk yet. Using fillers is a subconscious habit, so it's no surprise that they pop up in public speaking. Realise, though, that there's no need to hold space when you're public speaking. Even if public speaking is new to you, an audience automatically knows not to interrupt you, especially in a formal situation, so fillers are redundant.

2. Basically, like, actually repeating words that essentially don't actually mean much

The second set of clutter words are those that we repeat too often without knowing it. With some speakers, words like 'essentially', 'actually' and 'in fact' can reach epidemic levels.

Although I'm sure you've never been so inattentive, I've occasionally sat through a lecture tallying the number of times the speaker said 'basically'. That may be a fun game to play as an audience member, but if it happens to you as a speaker, you've lost your audience.

Notice the words or phrases that you use frequently. Ask yourself – do these words add value or clutter? Am I using them to add power, or as punctuation?

To help you, play the **UM Game** on p. 243.

V O I C E

E is for . . . Energy

Depending on your personality and the content of your speech, you may need to deliver a message with sincerity (e.g. a eulogy), authority (e.g. a management meeting presentation), drama (e.g. a motivating speech) or emotion (e.g. a wedding speech). But any style of message will be more powerful with energy behind it.

Energy is the amount of verbal oomph or self-belief you put into your performance. It's the degree to which you show that you're willing to 'stand up and be counted'. The energy of a performance will be affected by your use of intonation, gaps and volume, but there is also a special something that comes from focusing on energy as the fifth and final part of the VOICE model.

Imagine a speaker who's got it all right. He's got his eye contact, gestures, posture and movement pegged. His volume's spot on, he's throwing in gaps like an expert, his intonation rises and falls like a mountain range and there's not an 'um' in sight. But our speaker is still putting you off. Why? Because his vocal delivery lacks energy. Read Mr Lowe's toast out loud with the minimum of energy:

Mr Lowe – 'Hi everyone, I'm *very* pleased to welcome you here to the wedding of my daughter. Today is the most special day of my life since she was born. There's no gentleman to whom I would rather part with her than Jonathan.'

Without enough energy, a speaker with powerful or emotional words to deliver can come across as dull-witted, sarcastic or just plain boring. The words that come from a low-energy speaker run the risk of lacking credibility.

How do you develop energy?

1. First, check in with your body toolkit. How's your posture? Posture and energy are interrelated because, as mentioned before, posture affects the amount of oxygen you're taking in and oxygen affects your ability to be energetic when speaking. So check that your body is in a positive and relaxed position.

2. Back yourself as a public speaker. Believe that you can do the job and that people are interested in hearing you speak. The more confident you are in yourself, the more you'll allow your natural personality to show on stage and the higher your energy will be.

3. Now take ownership of your topic. Even if your topic was imposed, even if you were asked to stand in at the last minute and *unaccustomed as you may be* to public speaking, you are the person who is now representing your topic. If you show belief in your topic, your voice will exude energy. If you doubt your topic, your energy will drop and this will only reflect negatively on you.

4. Next, notice the energy levels of your audience. Your job as a speaker is not to match the audience's energy levels, but to bring them up slightly. It's not enough to just inform, audiences expect to be engaged and entertained.

5. Finally, channel any nerves or excitement into your voice. Allow passion to sparkle through, whatever you're saying.

But be careful not to overdo it. Imagine Ms High, who walks into an interview with a little too much energy:

Ms High – 'Hello everyone, hello, hello! Oh, hello! I'm soooo pleased to meet you all, this is all very, very exciting! Hello, hello, hello! I'm Ms High! Well, this is fabulous. I have to tell you how wonderful it is to be here and how lovely you all look. Oooh, let me shake you all by the hand! Hello!'

If Ms High keeps this up do you think she'll get the job? Keep your energy levels higher than your audience, but not so high that they hit the ceiling.

Awareness workout

☐ **Video your next public speaking encounter.** So many people have video phones these days that it's only down to you whether you see yourself speaking on video or not. It's a strange experience, but seeing yourself recorded is the fastest way to gain awareness of how your Speaker's Toolkit behaves.

☐ **Seek honest feedback from a colleague or other observer.** What are you doing to inspire and what embarrassing quirks does your speaking still possess?

☐ **Identify which parts of your Speaker's Toolkit are performing well and which need some work.** Choose the parts of your body and speech that you'd like to work on and write them down in your Ingredients List on p. 241.

☐ **Play the Um Game.** Turn to p. 243 for a game that will help you become more aware of your clarity of speech. Play it with friends or family.

☐ **Become master of your Speaker's Toolkit.** Over time, start to replace your old habits with an array of new and inspiring tricks. Turn up your impact with powerful pauses, daring shifts in volume and storytelling gestures.

Part

2

It's not how strongly you feel about your topic,
it's how strongly they feel about your topic
after you speak.

Tim Salladay

Edgar Mumble looked at the feedback forms from his audience and scratched his head. Then he frowned. 'Pah! How dare they say my talk was boring?' he scoffed, 'What do these people know anyway? I've studied this subject for 15 years. They were begging me to do the talk. They clearly haven't got a clue.' Edgar looked around the office to see if anyone was looking and slid the feedback sheets into the bin.

Empathy

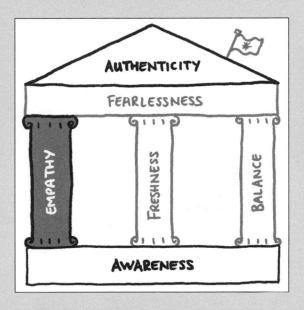

A powerful public speaker will engage the audience to the point where the audience embrace the topic as their own. Speakers with near magical amounts of empathy answer the audience's concerns and questions just as if they were mind readers. Then they have the audience buzzing with a feeling of 'Yes! That's me!' combined with the resonance of 'Wow! They can really help me with this!'

This is the cornerstone of really powerful public speaking. And yet so many presenters get it wrong. Their error goes right back to where they started, which is usually a list of the messages they want to get across, rather than thinking about what the *audience* want to hear. And all too often they'll start their presentation that way too. 'I'm here today to speak to you about . . .' – sound familiar?

What is perfect empathy?

- Knowing and understanding the needs of your audience.
- Recognising that your audience have surface level needs and hidden needs that they're hiding even from themselves.
- Understanding what your audience expects from the topic and what they hope for from you as a speaker.
- Managing those hopes, needs and expectations so that different types of audience members are satisfied.
- Bundling up all of this understanding and delivering it to the audience in a way that resonates with as many of them as possible.

With no empathy, a speaker ends up with an audience who are against them. Like Edgar Mumble's audience, this could mean silence and negative feedback. Or a lack of empathy could lead to awkward questions, rude comments and even people walking out of the room.

Why build empathy?

The concept of empathy needs a little more 'selling' than some of the other qualities in the Public Speaking House because so many speakers assume they know what their audience are thinking. More than this, an audience will rarely tell you, 'You really empathised with us, thank you', so it's difficult to get direct feedback about the effect empathy has on your listeners.

I occasionally come across speakers who decide that their preparation time is better spent on finding more facts, rather than working on building empathy towards their audience. If straightforward information is good enough to satisfy an audience, why *would* you work on the fuzzy and unfamiliar ground of empathy building?

Try it and you'll see. As you start to develop empathy with your audience you'll notice positive effects such as:

- Audience members listening more intently and contributing in ways that seem to further your aims.
- Indications that the audience relate to your message such as:
  - Shining eyes
  - Nodding
  - Strong eye contact
  - Laughter with your humour
  - Enthusiastic participation

- Comments in feedback forms like 'that was spot on', 'just what I wanted' and 'it answered all my questions'.
- Your own speaking experience feeling easier or more pleasant.

Time and again, it is the empathetic speaker who is remembered long after their speech. But don't just take my word for it. Research gives two reasons why empathy is so important. Social psychologists describe the feeling of closeness between an information giver (the speaker) and receiver (the audience) as 'immediacy'. If an audience feel more immediacy towards the speaker, they will learn more effectively.

Second, as developments in neuroscience are showing, there is a positive link between the emotional state of your audience and the amount they learn. In other words, happy audience members literally store and retain more information.

But a word of caution is needed. It's possible to be so 'matey' or informal that you are empathising with your audience at the expense of your material, e.g. sitting down in the audience when you should be speaking to everyone, or using brash language. This is not what we're aiming for. No matter how much you empathise with your audience, remember that you are still the speaker and that you have a job to do.

Empathy versus rapport

Notice that I've chosen to use the word 'empathy' rather than 'rapport'. Empathy is defined as 'understanding and entering into another's feelings'. Rapport is defined as 'a relationship of mutual understanding or trust and agreement between people'. Rapport is a give and take relationship, whereas empathy is giving understanding without expecting to receive any in return. We're all good at the 'me' part of a relationship, but typically neglect the 'they'. By focusing on empathy we redress that balance.

How do you develop empathy?

Developing empathy is a process of looking at public speaking in a different way. The shift from self-focus to audience-focus may be natural for you, or it may take some practice. Once you've learned this skill, it will remain strong. You will begin to know instinctively how to build empathy with an audience and your public speaking will benefit dramatically as a result.

This part focuses on the following tools to build empathy:

1. **Before you speak:**
   - Audience-focused Preparation.
   - Setting up your environment.
2. **During and after your talk:**
   - Setting agreements with your audience.
   - Different audience types and what to do with them.
   - Breaking rapport for impact.
   - Holding empathy beyond your performance.

Chapter

Preparing with empathy

Audience-focused Preparation

Audience-focused Preparation is a series of questions you can ask yourself about your audience's needs, hopes and expectations. The thought you put into preparation is your foundation for an empathetic presentation and is the basis for designing and delivering the talk your audience want to hear.

How much preparation do I need to do?

To start your Audience-focused Preparation, first ask yourself whether your speaking assignment is a low-risk or a high-risk occasion. This will determine how much you need to prepare.

LOW RISK   HIGH RISK

Are you speaking at a relaxed event, where your audience are on your side and will support you, whatever comes out of your mouth (low risk)?

Or is this an occasion with an important outcome, or an audience you want to impress, who have high expectations of 'how it should be done' (high risk)?

Once you know how much preparation is necessary, you can look at your speaking assignment from these three angles:

1. **The audience on the topic:** The expectations or preconceived ideas the audience hold about *your topic*.
2. **The audience on you:** The hopes your audience hold about how *you* will behave as a speaker.
3. **The audience on the audience:** The needs the audience hold towards *themselves* as individuals and as a group.

1. The audience on the topic

As soon as a speech, presentation or workshop is given a title, the individuals, who will later sit together as your audience, will be making a host of assumptions about how the topic will be.

There is a fantastic group which brings together highly inspirational speakers called TED. If you haven't come across them I really recommend a visit to their website www.ted.com.

Have a look at some of their recent talks and you'll get an idea of your gut reaction to different topics:

- 'What our hallucinations reveal about our minds.'
- 'On DNA and the sea.'
- 'Investing in Africa's own solutions.'
- 'A feminine response to Iceland's financial crash.'
- 'We can avoid aging.'
- 'A leap from the edge of space.'
- 'How to expose the corrupt.'
- 'Why not eat insects?'

Notice how some of these topics will interest you more than others? Some of them will sound fun, technical or intriguing and some you may know something about already. Your audience go through exactly the same process in judging your topic.

Consider what your audience know about your topic from the title and other information they may have about what you're going to say (such as a paragraph sent out with your speech title). Even if all your audience know is that your topic is 'The Best Man's Speech', there are still dozens of associations that instantly spring to mind:

Do your audience perceive the topic as exciting or boring? How many people will see this topic as important to them and how many are less concerned about it? How many people consider themselves beginners and how many think they're experts? Although you may not know for sure until you're in the room, these questions are designed to help you plan in the way that best empathises with the audience you anticipate.

You can find out more about your audience by:

- asking presenters who have faced a similar audience;
- asking members of your audience (if you are able to) what their expectations and assumptions are about the topic;

- finding out the 'popular opinion' about your subject from blog articles, newspapers, etc.

- asking the audience during your talk (risky if you do this alone);

- trial and error.

Look at the diagram below and ask yourself where your audience sit on each scale:

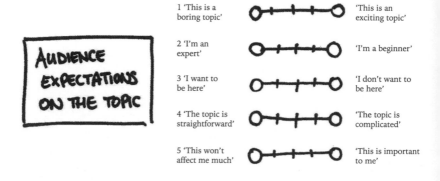

Once you've judged your audience's place on each scale, you will have a map of their expectations on the topic. The more you prepare, the better equipped you'll be to handle every situation you may face, even if there are some tricky characters in the audience (more on this later in Chapter 5).

Here's how you use the information from your audience expectation map to prepare or tailor your information.

1. Boring topic vs exciting topic

If you're presenting a topic that people usually consider boring, what can you do to change their minds? Use you Speaker's Toolkit (p.35) and develop Freshness (p.126) to jazz up your delivery. If people are likely to be excited by your topic, you have both a bonus and a possible danger. The bonus is that there will be a positive energy in the room and your audience will take less effort to energise. The danger is that if their expectations are not met and you deliver in a way that's less exciting than expected, you may disappoint.

Always aim to excite your audience in a way that's authentic to you. Excitement could mean bouncing around the stage enthusiastically, just as it could mean giving intelligent insight on a topic or invoking strong emotions through storytelling.

2. Experts vs beginners

It's crucial to know the knowledge level of your audience when you're delivering any kind of information-focused speech or presentation. If you pitch your content too low, your audience will leave feeling they've learned nothing. If you pitch too high, they'll be lost. Get it right and it will feel like you're exactly meeting their needs.

Sometimes it's easy to see the knowledge level of an audience, but if there are people at different knowledge levels you will need to stay flexible during your talk to see which level is the best for the group as a whole. Sometimes you'll have the opportunity to survey your audience on their knowledge levels and expectations for a talk, in which case treat that information as gold dust.

But if you have no way of researching your audience's expertise, then use your best guess to create a Plan A. Also prepare Plan B material that you can use if your audience have more, or less, knowledge than you thought. Before you launch into presenting your content, ask your audience some questions to judge their level. Try, 'How many of you have heard something about neurology before?' if you want a hands-up answer, or 'What do you know about neurology?' if you want more detailed information.

If your Plan A is wrong, it's now easy to adjust.

3. 'I want to be here' vs 'I'm only here because I have to be'

It's important to understand the likely motivation of your audience. Are your audience school children, employees or another group who have been forced to listen to you speak, or are they listening to you of their own accord? This will affect the degree to which you need to 'sell' the concept of your talk to them.

If you have an audience who have low motivation towards your topic, make sure that you get them involved in the topic as soon as possible. Find a way that works for you. I use fun and interaction a lot, especially when I work with young people (competitions and sweets work particularly well in this situation). Other speakers use colourful storytelling to show that this topic is relevant to the audience and others use their own brand of humour to get people interested. The important thing for low-motivation groups is to make them feel part of your talk. Show them how they fit into the topic.

For audiences who have chosen to hear you speak, reward and praise their enthusiasm. High-motivation groups can usually be relied upon to engage in lively discussion. Use their enthusiasm to go deeper into the material than you usually would – they will lap up any information you have to give them.

4. 'The topic is straightforward' vs 'The topic is complicated'

If many people in an audience perceive the topic as complicated, there may be an air of tension or confusion in the room, even before you start speaking. Mention accountancy, particle physics or property law to your average Joe and you'll see a reaction that indicates their discomfort with the subject.

It's important to get underneath this discomfort to see precisely what it relates to. Are they uncomfortable because they expect technical concepts that they don't understand? Are they uncomfortable because of the type of people involved with the profession? Where are they getting their information and stereotypes on your topic from?

This information will help you knock aside barriers to listening before they've even arisen in the minds of the audience. This is how some speakers seem to mind-read. They use the language of their audience to turn around the complexity of the subject into something they can relate to.

One accountant I know works with small, creative businesses. She starts her presentations with:

'We like you to think accountancy's difficult, but the secret is it's really a piece of cake. If we told you that, we wouldn't have a job!'

This instantly puts a tense audience at ease and allows them to soak up more information than if they were expecting not to understand the speaker.

You may have people at the other end of this spectrum, who think the topic is a piece of cake. In this case think about how you want to use that information. Perhaps you'd like to challenge them to see your topic isn't as set-in-stone as they think. Perhaps you'd like those who find it straightforward to help or work with others who struggle with the topic. Perhaps you'd prefer to split the audience into one group who find your topic simple and others who want to go at a slower pace. Think creatively about how best to serve their needs.

5. 'This is important to me' vs 'This won't affect me much'

An audience who think what you're saying is important to them will listen harder and for longer. So ask yourself what it is that your audience as a group really care about and then relate your topic to these things.

There was a fantastic example of this when finance guru Alvin Hall was brought in to teach maths to a group of disaffected teens. Rather then launch in with mathematical theory, he told them his rags to riches story from a childhood of crushing poverty to his current fame and fortune. When he linked this back to a basic understanding of maths you can bet he suddenly had their full attention.

So the steps for demonstrating importance of your topic are:

1. Using stories and examples to which your audience can relate.
2. Providing compelling reasons for them to find what you have to say important.
3. Using their language (whether they're teenagers or business managers) to get the message across.

Also, if you treat your topic as important, your energy will encourage the audience to feel the same way about it.

A friend of mine, Jack Butler of Future Foundations, is an outstanding motivational speaker for young people. He thinks carefully about his experiences as a child and relates them directly to his audience members. Using their language, their gestures and their ideas about the world, he's able to turn unimpressed inner-city teenagers into enthusiastic participants who then engage deeply in adult discussions because they see the relevance of what he's saying to them.

> **The audience on your topic**
>
> *Putting the picture together*
>
> Now you've established your audience's expectations of your topic, think how that affects your performance:
>
> - How much time should I take?
> - How much content is needed?
> - What are the best examples, anecdotes and 'fizzy bits' for my audience? (See Chapter 6.)
> - How do I need to frame the topic?
> - What else can I do to get this audience to relate to the topic?

2. The audience on you

As with a topic, any audience will hold a range of assumptions about you as a speaker. You have done it many times before towards other speakers, so don't worry, it's nothing personal. Read down this list of speakers to see the different reactions they can evoke, from 'Wow!' to 'Who?':

- Nelson Mandela
- George Bush
- Tanni Grey-Thompson
- Steve Jobs
- Marianne Williamson
- Steven Hawking

These are all speakers in the public eye, but the audience will apply similar judgement to you as a speaker. From the second you stand up to the moment you sit down, you give out signals about who you are as a speaker, what you stand for and what you will give to the audience. We looked at how your body and voice affect this in Part 1; now let's look at how you can empathise with the hopes your audience have about you as a speaker.

Exactly the same speech can be delivered in countless different ways by different speakers, depending on the personal touch that they bring. What will be your personal touch? How can you make sure it's the best one for empathising with your audience?

Ask yourself the following questions to get into your audience's mindset:

● What does my audience know about me?

● What will they assume about me because of what they already know?

● What would they ideally like me to do or say?

● What would they not like me to do or say?

● What would surprise or delight my audience about my performance?

These questions will point you towards your audience's hopes for you as their speaker. Now, map out their hopes on the diagram below to help you consider how best to empathise with them:

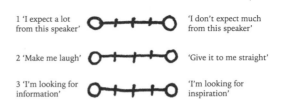

1 'I expect a lot from this speaker'   'I don't expect much from this speaker'

2 'Make me laugh'   'Give it to me straight'

3 'I'm looking for information'   'I'm looking for inspiration'

1. 'I expect a lot' vs 'I don't expect much from this speaker'

Even if you are not a public speaker, your audience will hold hopes for you based on what they know about you. This could be as abstract as 'Oh, she's wearing a bright green dress, this might be interesting', or as detailed as 'I've known Tony for 12 years and he's always the one to make a joke in the room, he should be great'. Or it could be the organisation or social group you're associated with that builds or crushes your reputation by proxy – 'He's from Amnesty, I love what they do,' or 'Uff, not another local government officer, do I really have to be here?'

If you have presented a few times or more, don't be surprised that word gets round. It's easy to develop a reputation as a very good speaker, just as it's easy to develop a reputation as a speaker who should be avoided at all costs. Your reputation will decide where the bar of your audience's hopes for you is set. If you've set the bar high in previous encounters, the audience will hope for the same again. Make sure you don't disappoint, by always striving to give all you can to your audience. If you've set the bar low, you may have just a few moments at the beginning of your talk to recapture their enthusiasm, before they switch off.

Your analysis of your reputation will reveal how you should deliver your speech or presentation. When you start your talk, think about how much you need to say to introduce yourself. What information will help you gain credibility? You can raise the hopes of your audience, or modestly lower them, by the right choice of words at the beginning.

What if . . . my audience don't like me?

Expert tip: Nigel Risner

Business coach, motivational speaker and author of *It's a Zoo Around Here*, Nigel Risner says that if you're worried about your audience liking you, always make sure you've got a great opening line. He says:

'Most people panic on their first line and start with the same meaningless waffle as everyone else: "Hello, thank you very much, my name's Nigel and it's a pleasure to be here."

'Get your audience on board with your first line and you're sorted. I often start with the question, "How many people in this room would like to have at least five per cent more success in some part of their life?", which starts my talk off on a "Yes". Find an opening line that guarantees a "Yes" answer from 90 per cent of your audience and half of the battle is won.

'Remember that in most speaking situations, 95 per cent of the audience want to love you, they're on your side. The remaining five per cent don't care how brilliant you are, they'll never like you. In every audience I speak to, five per cent want to marry me, five per cent want to kill me – it's bizarre. Acknowledge that this is all part of the game and focus on the 95 per cent who like you.

2. 'Make me laugh' vs 'Give it to me straight'

Are you delivering a speech, a toast or a workshop? Are you likely to have reverent faces staring at you, or are your audience clutching glasses of champagne and waiting to be entertained? The occasion, combined with your knowledge about your audience's other needs and expectations, will point to how much humour your audience are likely to be hoping for in your performance.

In many public speaking situations an audience will prefer to be made to laugh, even if it's gentle, reflective humour at a funeral. Humour can be used to diffuse a tense situation, to build a sense of group cohesion, or to entertain.

On some occasions, however, humour will be perceived in a negative light by an audience. Imagine an air hostess cracking a joke about flight safety, or a royal poking fun at the ambassador in front of a large audience. There's a time and a place to make the audience laugh and it's up to you to both judge what your audience is *likely* to hope for and to read the room as you're speaking. See Chapter 6 for more on humour.

3. Information vs inspiration

In some situations such as a lecture, a business meeting or an announcement, you have crucial information to deliver. Here, *what* you say is more important than *how* you say it. On other occasions, such as toasts and speeches, it's the inspiration you leave the audience with that is more important than the specifics of the content.

Speakers use all sorts of tools – photos, videos, interactive games, props, acting, etc. – to get across their message (more on these tools later, in Chapters 6 and 7), but it's up to you to choose the balance wisely to build the maximum amount of empathy with your audience.

If your talk is factual, use these tools to support and re-emphasise your factual message. Just because you have a factual message doesn't mean that this must translate into a generic PowerPoint presentation. Ask yourself what your audience *really* want from a factual speech or presentation. They are probably looking for 'Aha!' moments where they understand the topic more effectively, or have learned a new way of applying it to themselves. How can you as a speaker maximise the chance of 'Aha'?

If your audience are hoping for an emotional delivery, step up and give them as much as you have. Support your delivery with photographs, videos and other media that evoke the appropriate emotion. Audiences with these hopes love to see their speaker being deeply honest, so soul-search a little to find a touching and authentic way to deliver your message. For example, a groom could spend 15 minutes telling his wedding party how happy he is that he has married Sophie. Or he could say nothing and instead, with the audience focused on him, slowly and delicately pull out a tiny pair of baby socks to give to his new wife. Which do you think would best empathise with the group's needs?

4. Just how I like it

Other hopes the audience may have of you relate to the way you manage a speaking engagement. These include the length of speech – 'Keep it short and sweet' vs 'You should be thorough' and the amount of audience involvement – 'I just want to listen' vs 'I want to be involved'.

The audience may not consciously be aware of their own hopes, so it's up to you to figure out what would really go down well for your listeners, based on everything else you know about them. If they're likely to be an impatient audience, get through your material succinctly, then give them a chance to ask questions (if appropriate). If your audience have that 'first day of term' enthusiasm, you might increase the amount of content you put in. If they are a quiet or nervous audience, expect either to have to talk more or to make more effort to get them involved.

The audience on you

Putting the whole picture together

Now you know more about what your audience want from you, you can take some more decisions about how to speak:

- How do my audience want me to be as a speaker?
- How do they want me to relate to my material?
- How much humour should I be using?
- Should I focus on information or emotions?

3. The audience on the audience

Finally, it's worth briefly mentioning the needs that come from how the audience view themselves, as individuals and as a group. Imagine you were in the following group situations. How would you feel? How would you react to the other members of your group? What would you need from the speaker to help you make the most of their public speaking?

- Listening to a church sermon.
- You, the adult, listening to the teacher along with a classroom of 6-year-olds.
- Participating in a pitch at a sales meeting.

- Watching a comedian at the Hammersmith Apollo.
- Sitting in a large conference room listening to a speaker who fascinates you.

Perhaps as a member of a congregation you'd want your faith or lack of faith to be recognised. Perhaps as an adult in the classroom, you'd like the teacher to treat you differently to the 6-year-olds. And perhaps whilst watching a comedian you'd desperately like to stay anonymous, rather than become the butt of his jokes. These needs may be shared by other members of the audience, but not necessarily all of them. Here it is important to start noticing common threads that run through all or different parts of your audience.

Get under the skin of your audience. As individuals, do they secretly yearn to be recognised as intelligent? Important? Are they nervous, but want to feel confident? Do they long to be seen as good at what they do? Do they see themselves as party animals? Good, honest people? How many of them feel lonely or isolated in the room? Choose the characteristics your audience would be most likely to associate with and be sure to talk to them as if they already possess these qualities. This is a sure way of tickling their empathy buttons. Here are a few ideas of how that might look.

An audience needing to be recognised as 'good, honest people'

'I can see we all care deeply about this. And the spirit of understanding within this room is deeply impressive.'

NB: the repetition of 'deeply' acknowledges the depth or maturity of the audience.

An audience needing to be recognised as confident

'As I walked into this room, I felt an air of expectation. "Can I make it through this year?" "Is it going to be as difficult as everyone says?" Well. I know that you can do it. You know you can do it. We know that we can do it.'

NB: Positive language and the repetition of 'can do it' builds confidence.

An audience with a high number of people feeling lonely

'We all know how daunting a new environment can be. Take a look around you at all the new and diverse faces in the room. There's so much to learn from each other. Now, catch someone by the eye, shake their hand and tell them, "Well done for being here".'

NB: this example skilfully draws together lonely members of the group and gives them an 'ice-breaking' connection to another audience member.

The audience on the audience
Putting the whole picture together

Based on the audience's image of themselves and as a group, ask yourself:

● What language should I use to relate to the audience?
● What do they want me to see in them as individuals, or as a group?
● What sort of ice-breaking activities are needed?
● How will the group respond to interactive exercises?

Setting up your environment

The next part of developing empathy is to understand how the environment in which you're speaking affects the audience. As a speaker, you're often in charge of how you manage your room to get the most out of it. Don't assume that because a room is set up in a certain way you have to stick to it. So long as you arrive at the room in advance, there are usually a number of things you can do to set up shop in a way that will best suit the needs of your audience.

Layout

You can see the power of room layout by comparing the Houses of Commons to a theatre such as Shakespeare's Globe. The Commons, with its two 'audiences' facing each other, encourages participation from all, whereas the Globe focuses everyone's attention on the stage and asks the audience to listen. There are four room layouts most commonly used in public speaking situations:

1. **Horseshoe (10 to 30 people):**
   Perfect for small groups where your audience would benefit from interacting with each other. This is my preferred setup for workshops because it gives you and your audience a lot of space to move about in. A horseshoe can also work for larger audiences if you have a big room.

Horseshoe layout

2. **Theatre (50 to 500+ people):** Good where you want to pack your audience in and have the attention focused on you as speaker.

Theatre layout

3. **Boardroom (2 to 25 people):** This style works for small meetings and workshops where people need to write. You'll often find business meetings, especially more lengthy ones, in this room format. If you need a larger audience to write, theatre style with tables can work well.

Boardroom layout

4. **Cabaret (50 to 150+ people):** Dinner tables with six people seated around them allow enough room for the audience to all see the speakers without craning their necks. This format is ideal for gala dinners and weddings.

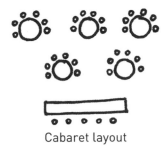

Cabaret layout

What if . . . I'm nervous about speaking to a large audience?

Expert tip: Derek Williams

'I used to be terrified of public speaking,' says Derek Williams, who today is an inspirational speaker on customer service. 'One day I asked myself, "I'm not afraid to speak to one person, so why am I afraid to talk to a whole audience?"

'I decided that since they are only listening to one person, I would only speak to one person too. I developed a method of speaking to one member of the audience for 15 seconds at a time. I like having conversations with people, so that felt fine. The bigger the audience was, the more I told myself, "Wow – look at all the conversations I can have today!" Twenty years on, I can handle any size of audience. An added benefit is that all that eye contact creates a really personal feeling in my audience, so the feedback I get is that my audiences feel really engaged.'

Once you've got the hang of a standard room setup, think about how you might use your layout to create a more memorable experience for your audience, based on their needs:

- If you want your workshop group to feel more together, connect the ends of your horseshoe to make a circle.

- For a theatre setup that signals 'dynamic' to the audience, curve in some of the chairs at the front to be more surrounded by the audience.

- Deliberately change the end you'll speak from in your boardroom to show the audience 'we're going to think differently now'. You'll be surprised how different it feels for the audience to be looking at a new piece of wall. It feels like breaking the rules and they'll love you for it!

- Instead of standing at the top table, why not move through your audience as you speak to a cabaret-style room? Microphone permitting, this could be a good way to satisfy the audience's hopes to connect with their speaker.

Sitting in their seats

Even if you have an event manager organising your speaking engagement, take responsibility for the experience of your audience by checking some environmental factors that are critical to their enjoyment. Start by sitting in a few of the seats the audience will occupy and ask yourself some questions from their point of view:

- What can I see? Are there any distractions that will take the audience's attention away from the you? Windows, moving objects, or interesting things to read behind your stage may pull attention away from you whilst you're speaking.

- What does the setup say about the speaker? You can reinforce your key messages by placing relevant props or visual aids on stage for the audience to see as they come into the room. Many speakers use presentation banners, but equally you could use a model skeleton, a flag, or a mop and brush as part of your stage setup – whatever would link with your message. Props are a great idea if your audience are open to a bit of fun (more on props in Chapter 6).

- How comfortable is it to sit here? Is the temperature of the room too hot or too cold? Conference delegates often sit shivering in rooms with air conditioning, when the speaker could easily put them out of their misery by having it turned down.

- What other noises, quirks of the room, or other environmental factors do I notice? Pick up these small pieces of information about your audience's experience, so that when you're speaking you can relate to and refer to what they're experiencing, rather than to your own environment on stage which will be very different. A quick comment like 'Oof, it's cold in here – I'm afraid the heating's broken, so we'll all have to battle through' will show your audience that you empathise with their needs.

Chapter

5

Managing the crowd

Now we turn to empathising with your audience as you speak. You've prepared by developing bundles of empathy with who you think your audience are, so how do you now use that preparation in reality?

Setting agreements with your audience

Spend some time in the first few minutes of your talk setting agreements with your audience. This is a process of clarifying exactly what you and the audience want to get from your talk. If your speech is only a few minutes, either do this process very speedily or leave it out.

Use your Audience-focused Preparation to tell you what your audience need you to clarify or 'put in the room' before you leap into your content. Remember to voice any agreements that need to be made around:

- What they should expect from the **topic**.
  - What's important about the topic.
  - What you are going to talk about.
- What they should expect from you as the **speaker**.
  - How much time you are likely to spend.
  - What style you will use.
- You recognising who they are and what they need as an **audience**.

There are two simple methods for setting agreements, as follows.

Method 1: Short and sharp

For: speeches, large groups or authoritative monologues.

1. **Show the audience what you know about them.**

   'We have an élite in this room. Renowned doctors/lawyers/ scientists [agreement for an audience who need to be seen as intelligent]. *I'm really grateful for an hour of your time* [agreement on time]. *I've already had a lot of questions from you about my topic, so I'm honoured to be presenting you with information that's both current and relevant to your work* [agreement on topic]. *And because we're all busy people, my guess is that you'd appreciate as much information as possible from me in the time we have together* [agreement on speaker style – 'I'll give lots of information'].

2. **Check that this is true.**

   'Does this sound good to you?'

   If you receive a resounding 'Yes!', move down to point three. If it doesn't come, or you sense from the audience that they were hoping for something else, adjust your agreement with the audience:

   'No problem, it looks like some of you have different hopes from me. I want you all to leave here with what you came for, so I'll be sure to leave a good length of time at the end for your questions.'

3. Now show them how you've tailored what you're going to say to their specific needs.

   'Great, let's jump in. Those of you who have seen me speaking before will know that I like to use video clips in my presentations [agreement on speaker style] *so let's kick off with this one . . .'*

This method is useful if you have a specific message you want to deliver, if you know your audience well, or if you are pressed for time.

Method 2: Building in-depth audience buy-in.

For: workshops, group work, and question and answer sessions, where the focus is on the audience learning and growing together. This method is a way of giving power to your audience, so they feel they've agreed what the content of your session should be. This will help the audience listen and retain information more effectively and it will reflect well on you.

1. **Briefly show the audience what you know about them.**

   'You're a group of intelligent, enthusiastic people here' [agreement on audience needs].

2. **Get permission to make agreements.**

   'I'd like you to help me shape the time we have together, so we can cover as many of the things you need as possible.'

3. **Brainstorm audience expectations and hopes.**

   'I'd like you to tell me what's most important for us to cover today. What are your questions for me about the topic?' [agreements on topic].

   Brainstorm:

   'And now, we might like to make some agreements about how we work together as a group. Would you like me to share my own stories? Would you like lots of time to work together? How can we make this work best for you?' [agreements on speaker style].

   This section can take a lot of time if you let it. If you need to keep it short and sharp, ask each member of the audience to give one idea.

4. **Get the audience to prioritise their collective expectations and hopes.**

'We seem to have a long list of requirements from you here. Which would you see as the priorities? Which can we let slip?'

Sometimes you will find competing hopes within the audience, e.g. one person wants to 'Keep it short term' and another wants to 'Look long term'. Allow the audience to decide where they as a group would like to focus their attention.

5. **Trim and agree.**

'Here's our shortlist of what you'd like to get from the session. Most of this is right in line with my own expectations. We'll probably get through most of these three main points today, but do you mind if I let this point slip? It's a complex subject that I think would distract from our purpose, so instead I'll give you some suggested reading on it, OK?'

Here, use your experience to show the audience what's best for them. If there is a topic or question you don't want to cover that has been brought up, make it clear that you won't be covering it and explain why. 'That's outside my area of expertise', 'That goes in a different workshop' or 'We don't have time to cover this section' are all credible reasons for trimming. Agreeing this openly is crucial for demonstrating empathy and avoiding disappointment.

6. **Now show them your plan and how it fits with what they want.**

'And this is the structure I propose for you today. I hope you can see we've got most of your points factored in, and then these other smaller points I can cover in the question and answers at the end. Does that sound good?'

This process can take a few minutes if you have a session that's only an hour or two, or it can take much longer if your group will be working with you for a number of days.

Once you've done this with a few audiences, you'll notice common questions and expectations from them. This information is gold dust that you can use to empathise more accurately with your next audience.

Different audience types and how to handle them

Back in 1970 Richard Mann and his colleagues created a model of eight different audience types a teacher experiences in a college classroom. Below is my reworking of their brilliant model to help you get an understanding of the different characters you might experience in an audience.

1. The Sheep

- Sheep are conventional, focused on what you're saying and look to you for the answers. They rarely question your control.

- They listen hoping to understand the material and often prefer a lecture to a discussion. Sheep speak out only to agree or to ask clarifying questions.

- Sheep are unlikely to show independence or creativity. They might find creative questions and tasks more difficult than others, so clear instructions are important.

If you have a room full of Sheep: You'll get the feeling of being rather important, just like a shepherd to a flock. You will notice an atmosphere of respect and perhaps reverence. This is common in large, adult audiences, where there is a high level of desire to hear what you have to say. Don't worry if eye contact is limited: it's probably because your fluffy white Sheep are busy taking notes.

How to handle Sheep: Sheep will feel like your allies. You can also use them to chip in on your side if you're asked a difficult or negative question. If you're struggling with holding an audience it could be because you lack Sheep. Turn other audience types into compliant Sheep by illustrating what you and the audience have in common. Keep them following you by demonstrating your authenticity; for example, don't pretend to know the answer to a question if you don't know. If Sheep pick up on the vibes of inauthenticity, they'll stop trusting you and wander off elsewhere. If you want to stimulate your Sheep into a more active role, encourage them to make critical comments and to contribute to discussions.

2. The Hotshot

Hotshots are comfortable and confident members of the audience.

- They listen intently to what you have to offer, whilst keeping in mind their own learning goals at the same time.
- Hotshots love seminar or discussion formats and are high-level participators.
- They make friends with the speaker easily and take responsibility for their own learning.
- Hotshots learn quickly and will ask challenging questions to deepen their learning, or to clarify their understanding.
- If you're not performing as the audience hoped and there is the time and social dynamic to make a complaint or suggestion, Hotshots may be the ones to act as spokesperson for the group's concerns.

If you have a room full of Hotshots: Your audience will seem engaged, participative, positive and challenging. Discussions will flow easily and insightful comments will arise naturally. An audience like this will quickly know if you are confident in your topic or haven't prepared enough.

How to handle Hotshots: Prepare your topic well. Acknowledge their independence – 'I can tell you've thought a lot about this subject and thank you for that' – and encourage them to push beyond what is expected of other audience types. Use questions to bring out their insight and include interactive activities that help them learn individually and from the group. If you don't know the answer to their question, don't fake it. Tell them it's a good question and either take it offline – ('Speak to me about it after'), say you'll find out for them (and make sure you do), or bounce it back to the audience ('Honestly, I don't know. Can anyone in the audience help?' or 'What do you think?'). Hotshots will be keen to soak up your information, so make them aware if handouts are coming at the end, or allow them the time to note down key points.

3. The Clown

- Clowns love the social part of listening to a public speaker and this is often more important to them than absorbing information.

- They're chatty and often offer lively comments and questions to entertain, rather than to support the speaker.

- Clowns love discussion and interactive exercises and are often the leaders in group work.

- If treated well, Clowns are pleasant to have in an audience and capable of focusing well if they see others concentrating.

- Clowns are easy to motivate by giving them attention.

If you have a room full of Clowns: There will be a bubbly, lively atmosphere, but the feel will be different from a room full of Hotshots. Here you will face more off-topic stories, jokes and in-conversations. This can result in anything from fun to frustration, depending on how you manage your Clowns.

How to handle Clowns: Use their social skills in group discussions and interactive exercises, but keep your Clowns on track by asking very specific questions and cutting short any irrelevant/waffly comments. Avoid being too serious with them or you'll seem pompous. Laugh with their joke, allow the audience to enjoy it and then pull the focus back onto your topic. If you need them to be calmer or more serious, get them on track gently by mentioning the purpose of your talk or meeting, saying how you want the audience to behave and giving them a time expectation for the remainder of the talk.

Use a light, positive touch with Clowns. Avoid confronting them, or restricting their freedom to participate – this can lead to a frustrated Clown. If they become frustrated with you as a speaker, they can turn into the dreaded Sniper (below).

Also, make sure you avoid getting distracted from other audience types just because your Clowns are entertaining and noisy. Channel their energy to contribute towards your message.

Audience types: the Sheep, the Sniper and the Black Cloud

4. The Sniper

- Snipers start out with a hostile or cynical attitude towards you or your topic.

- Snipers are often switched on and listening out for an opportunity to criticise or show their expertise in the room.

- They have strong attention spans and can be used well for discussions where critical analysis is important.

- This is often the person you fear in question and answer sessions. Don't let the Sniper take over the room with their questions and don't forget they are just one person.

If you have a room full of Snipers: You'll notice an atmosphere of competition and aggression; individuals trying to win a point or show themselves to be most intelligent. Arms may be folded or eyes rolled as you start to speak. Preparation and confidence are very important when handling this personality type.

How to handle Snipers: First of all, recognise your own expertise – you are standing at the front of the room for a reason. Snipers are only a problem if you're feeling uncomfortable – otherwise they can't hurt you. Although snipers may sound personal, remember that the Sniper doesn't want to cause you pain, they want an answer to their question. Avoid taking their bullet yourself by directing the snipe back to the topic in hand, to see if the Sniper's view of the world is legitimate. It may well be. Refer to the topic as 'ours', so that you are discussing rather than defending your standpoint.

Speaker [jovially] – 'As we've all experienced, alcohol is usually needed before British gentlemen are able to express their emotions!'

Sniper [angrily] – *'Yes, but you're wrong, aren't you? I proposed to my wife sober. I talk emotionally to her all the time. I don't even drink.'*

Speaker [calmly] – *'Thanks for sharing. [To the whole audience]*
What do you think? Does that make our rule invalid, or is it the exception that proves the rule?'

Welcome the comments, rather than battling them, or you will only stoke the Sniper's fire. Resist the temptation to try and 'win' the argument. Provide reasonable and tangible evidence to support your point and leave it at that. Often Snipers' energy will fizzle out if they are left unprovoked.

What if . . . an audience member is really rude to me?

Expert tip: Nick Williams

'Harsh feedback cannot always be avoided', says Nick Williams from www.inspired-entrepreneur.com, who has 20 years' experience inspiring entrepreneurs through his public speaking. But don't let the fear of that stop you doing anything. If rudeness comes your way, then:

1 'Don't take it too personally – you may well have hit some-one's emotional hot button – but it is *their* hot button, not yours. Allow them to have their thoughts and feelings.

2 Be aware of your own emotional hot buttons – judgement or criticism can lead you to feel hurt, angry or defensive. Don't resist this, but be willing to explore those feelings and develop ways of "desensitising" yourself.

3 Anticipate what you fear – think through the questions, statements or challenges you might dread getting thrown at you and imaging what you'd say, how you'd feel and what you'd think in response. By preparing you feel more confi-dent and less defensive.

▶

'I have used my years of speaking, broadcasting and being interviewed as a "personal growth" path. Many of my hot buttons have been triggered over the years, and my goal is to use them as great self-awareness and giving me insights into places where I need to do some inner work so I am less defensive and more open. Over time, I have aimed to develop my character, rather than use clever tips or techniques – it seems to have worked for me.'

5. The Snowman

- No matter how much you talk to a Snowman (in real life, or in your audience), they won't respond. Snowmen are highly socially anxious and do not speak during interactive exercises, but they're very aware of how the speaker behaves towards them.

- This anxiety can come from a fear of speaking in public, or a lack of confidence in their knowledge. They convince themselves that if they ask a question, everyone will think badly of them and decide it's better to stay silent.

- Snowmen often secretly desire a close relationship with the speaker, but are afraid because the speaker seems more important than them.

- Snowmen are often found in technical specialities and professions where human contact is infrequent or unimportant.

If you have a room full of Snowmen: You'll notice that it's very difficult to get a reaction from them – questions and interactive exercises will feel laboured. Eye contact may be limited as Snowmen prefer not to be picked on to speak.

How to handle Snowmen: The biggest mistake you can make is to ignore the Snowmen. As I've mentioned before, it's important to make sure every participant receives attention. Do this by smiling at individuals, walking to their part of room, making eye contact and so on. Create a welcoming atmosphere and they'll participate in your activities. Start with interactivity that's within their comfort zone – e.g. a 'Pair Share' – see p. 138. Another method is to have everyone in a group say a word or sentence to contribute to a brainstorm. That way the Snowman has a chance to be involved.

Snowmen are often the most reflective members of an audience. Because of their detachment from the group they can offer useful insights into the topic, if you directly ask them for their opinion.

6. The Black Cloud

- The Black Cloud is characterised by their negative body language, such as frowning, wandering eyes, folded arms or slumped shoulders. Take care when judging this audience type, because an audience member who is frowning may just be concentrating hard.

- They hold a resigned, 'can't-do' attitude to themselves with respect to the subject matter. They believe it is a tricky, boring or irrelevant subject.

- Black Clouds take more energy to motivate than others and are easily bored.

- Turned off by typical ways of presenting, the Black Cloud has probably 'seen it all before' and decided they don't like it or can't do it.

- Black Clouds can also be other audience types who, after a long day of listening to unimpressive speakers, are tired of listening.

If you have a room full of Black Clouds: You'll notice low energy, slumped body language and low resonance with what you're saying. Black Clouds will have a glazed look in their eyes – provided they haven't seen something interesting out of the window.

How to handle Black Clouds: Start by explaining the ways in which your message differs in style or method of delivery to the usual explanation on the matter. If your room is full of Black Clouds, get some energy flowing with movement or interactivity, taking care to explain why you're doing it – 'We're going to have some interesting discussions today, so let's first get to know each other better by playing a short game.'

Bring some sunshine to your Black Clouds by showing extra enthusiasm towards your subject, so they get carried along. If you drop down to their energy level, everyone will leave the room depressed. Recognise that the subject may be difficult for them and offer reassurance that you can change that for them. Once on-board, compliment and encourage the Black Cloud on any input they give to a session. Offer them supportive and energetic gestures and eye contact to show that the subject matter isn't as deadly serious as they may have thought.

7. The Unwanted Panellist

- This is the 'expert' in the room who hasn't been asked to present.

- Similar to the Clown, the Unwanted Panellist has a high degree of confidence, but they lack respect for, or awareness of, the social protocol expected in the group.

- The Unwanted Panellist will frequently try to add to your knowledge by trying to teach the audience from their own experience. This can sometimes be a deliberate attempt to win business or respect from the audience.

- They are often the first to answer a speaker's questions and speak for longer than is desired.

- The Unwanted Panellist is seen by other members of the audience as irritating, pushy or distracting.

If you have a room full of Unwanted Panellists: There's usually only space for a couple of Unwanted Panellists in the room. But if there are more your talk or workshop will feel really out of control, with people chipping in with competing stories and ideas all over the place. Unwanted Panellists create friction with audience members who came to hear you speak, so it's up to you to minimise the disturbance they cause.

How to handle the Unwanted Panellist: Ideally you should have no Unwanted Panellists in the room; they should either stay silent or speak in places that are appropriate. To help this happen, build the right agreements before you start the main body of your talk. Try agreements like 'Let's come to this room with an open mind and leave whatever outside knowledge and experience we have outside the door', or 'Let's agree to give everyone an equal chance to talk in the room. Nobody should hog the floor space too much'.

If your Unwanted Panellist continues to perk up, judge what the rest of your audience need. If they're causing prickles of frustration, remind them that you are the speaker in the room and that if they have more to say you'd be happy to discuss it afterwards. Speak firmly but calmly and your audience will thank you for it.

What if . . . I get an awkward question from my audience?

Expert tip: Mamta Saha

'Mindset is very important when answering awkward questions,' says psychologist Mamta Saha from www.think spalondon.com. 'You have to believe the audience are on your side. Before you speak, tell yourself that any questions you get from the audience are coming from a place of "wanting to understand" your content, not from wanting to trip you up.

'If you are already dreading the thought of people asking you questions before you speak, you naturally create an uncomfortable anxiousness in yourself and the audience, who will be quick to pick up and respond to this anxiety. If you stay calm and approach questions in a positive way you keep your audience engaged and maintain your confidence throughout.

'When an awkward question is asked, summarise it to yourself in your mind and then repeat it back to the audience in your own words. This shows that you "hear" what they are saying and allows you to check your understanding. In the meantime, you have a little space to process the question. You are then in a position to share your insights on the question, form an opinion and share your thoughts.

'If you still need more time, you might say "this is a very interesting stance", which gives you an opportunity to open the question up to the audience. You could go on to invite the audience to comment. As you they speak, you will find your own expertise to add.'

Holding empathy with your audience beyond your performance

If you would like to have an ongoing relationship with your audience, holding empathy beyond the room where you spoke is crucial. Here's how.

1. Invite feedback

If you've delivered a long talk or workshop, get the audience to complete an evaluation form. Ask them for specific feedback on the areas you'd like more information about, e.g.:

- In general, how did you feel about the topic before you came to this workshop?
- How do you feel about this topic now?
- Which parts of the workshop met your needs?
- Which parts were less relevant to you?
- What would you change about this workshop?
- What did you like about the speaker's style and approach?
- What could be improved about the speaker's style and approach?

Choose questions carefully to get the most relevant information in the short time you will have left of the audience's attention span. Then, take away the feedback and look at it from an impersonal standpoint. Avoid getting caught up on anything too positive or too negative. Look at what you can do next time to better serve your audience.

2. The aftermath

- Stick around after you've finished speaking to answer any questions. If you have a crowd battling to speak to you, well done – you've hit a nerve with them.
- As personal branding expert Lesley Everett advises, be the same 'you' on stage and off stage. If you are bubbly and friendly when speaking but scowl at an audience member 'I'm busy' as you leave the room, you will break the good feeling you built up whilst you were talking.

3. Follow up

- Follow up on anything you've promised to do during your talk. It's easy to let things slide when the adrenaline of speaking is gone, but following up your commitments will show the audience that you're trustworthy. Even if you never see that audience member again, they will spread the word that you are a speaker to be trusted.

- Where appropriate, be sure to get the contact details of your audience members and follow up with an email, a thank you or a resource from your talk. This is especially important when you're hoping to generate business from speaking.

Empathy workout

- ☐ **Do your Audience-focused Preparation.** Use the questions from this chapter and your own analysis of your audience's needs to work out what they expect from you as a speaker, based on your topic, and their own esteem needs as an audience.

- ☐ **Tailor your performance to your Audience-focused Preparation.** With your new understanding of your audience's needs, how can you adjust your content, delivery style and techniques to benefit them as much as possible?

☐ **Practise using your speaking environment to alter what the audience experience**. Use a different room layout to give a different message to your audience.

☐ **Learn to handle different types of audience members**. Observe the different types of individuals in the next audience you experience, whether you're in the audience or speaking to them. Which characters do you recognise from this chapter? What could you do to best satisfy their needs?

☐ **Wrap up in style**. Challenge yourself to hold empathy after your next public speaking performance, both with the audience immediately after you've finished and by contacting them afterwards with follow-up information.

Part

3

They may forget what you said, but they
will never forget how you made them feel.

Carl W. Buechner

Suzie Talkalot peered down at her long list of bullet points, then up at her audience. Even Ben – *best mate, enthusiastic Ben* – was slumped down in his seat, checking his phone. Suzie didn't mind public speaking when she was first asked, but she soon realised that people just don't like to listen.

She sighed. 'Why do I always have to be the one that presents the boring information?' she asked herself.

Freshness

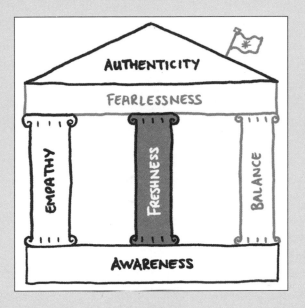

If it were possible to commit a public speaking crime, it would be subjecting your audience to dull, passionless public speaking. How often have you heard speakers begin with an apology: 'Sorry, I won't take very long' or 'Sorry, it isn't very interesting'?

How many times have you sat in an audience, framing a handout with elaborate doodles whilst a speaker drones on and on? How many times have you endured a presentation with the same old PowerPoint format? You know the one . . . it has a company logo, a title, four or five neat bullet points and, if you're lucky, a small picture in one corner 'to add some fun'.

Aside from being life-sapping for your audience, public speaking that lacks freshness lacks memorability. Neuroscience shows that we remember information more effectively when our mind and senses are engaged. Yet still thousands of audiences every day sit passively listening as a speaker talks.

Well, this will not happen to your audience! Part 3 outlines the tools you can use to give your presentations that fizz of Freshness which will make every audience sit up, pay attention and – most importantly – remember what you've said.

What is perfect Freshness?

- Surprising your audience with innovative, authentic and inspiring moments.
- Creating a **public speaking experience** for the audience, rather than just another talk to listen to. A public speaking experience means that the audience are engaged in what you're saying; they're *experiencing* it, rather than passively watching your talk (and worse, wishing it were over).

- Being comfortable to change the normal routine. It could be adding more energy and excitement, or it could be adding moments of silence and intensity.
- Selecting the right visual, verbal and interactive tools to make your impact.
- Finding that individuals coming back to you months or years later to say, 'I remember when you did/said that . . .'

The science bit

The hippocampus is the part of the brain that is associated with remembering facts and events. Those facts are later transferred to our cortex, the part of the brain responsible for creating rules and long-term memory. The aim of public speaking, then, is to get your information into your audience's hippocampi. To do this you need to make sure your information is both novel and significant.

How do you develop Freshness?

Once you have decided *what* to say through your Audience-focused Preparation, it's time to add the colour and sparkle to *how* you say it. During this part, we'll focus on three areas to help you bulk up your freshness:

1. **Vibrant Visuals:** Taking a fresh perspective on how to use visual aids.
2. **Wonderful Words:** Becoming a master on verbal techniques
3. **Ingenious Interactivity:** Involving your audience in what you do.

Get fresh

But before we start on the specifics, you need to step into a new mindset regarding your public speaking. This is a mindset in which you are not a public *speaker* who's delivering a talk, but a public *engager* who's delivering an *experience* to your audience. To do this you'll need bravery and creativity. Here's how you get there.

1. Start by resetting your attitude

When we are children we think anything is possible: 'I want to be an astronaut', 'I'm going to live in a palace,' and so on. As we grow up, we acquire rules about what's really possible and how we should behave. Eventually, we get into the world of work and we're encouraged to 'leave our personalities at reception desk, please'.

In this context, it's little wonder that so many people are afraid to step outside the norm of public speaking. As so much of life is based on playing a social role, or hiding or moderating the authentic you, your sense of Freshness may feel very rusty indeed. For some, it may seem difficult to so much as smile as they speak, let alone add freshness.

To get fresh, you're going to need a fresh attitude and allow those hidden, childlike thoughts to get through. Remove any sign of thoughts like:

'I *have* to do this'

'They won't be interested'

'I better just get through this'

'Everyone else does their public speaking like this . . . [using PowerPoint, a certain format or a certain style], so I should too'

'My audience will probably be bored, but that will have to be OK'

and replace them with thoughts that encourage freshness:

'I *want* to do this'

'I'm going to make sure they find this interesting'

'I'm going to be playful and enjoy this speaking opportunity'

'This is my opportunity to try something new and learn from it'

'My audience will be engaged and challenged and that's great!'

If you plan a talk with the second list of thoughts in your head, it will automatically become fresher.

2. Get creative

We understand surprisingly little about how creativity is acquired. Cognitive scientist Paul Thagard makes the best suggestion I've come across, a list of habits highly creative people employ, based on the habits of successful scientists. To get creative he advises:

1. **Make new connections:** Don't just use the same old material to create your talk. Look for inspiration from a different field of knowledge and use analogies to link things together.
2. **Don't be afraid of failure:** If you are afraid of doing something wrong, you will restrict your ability to try. Failure is just a sign that you're trying something new and pushing your boundaries, so make it your aim to fail!
3. **Be persistent:** Give your new, fresh style a chance to succeed, even if it feels uncomfortable or hits some problems at the start.
4. **Get excited:** Nothing is fresher than enthusiasm, so try looking at your topic through the eyes of an excited puppy. What do you like about your topic? Why is it important? What thrilling insight will your talk reveal?

5. **Be sociable:** Creative ideas come best when you have new influences, so look to others for ideas about how you can do something different. You could try speaking with a partner to see how that freshens up your performance.

6. **Use the world:** There is inspiration all around you, every moment of your life, if you're just open to it. Seek ideas, metaphors, stories and humour from the world at large. Bring the richness of your experience into your public speaking.

Creativity is a journey, not a destination. Expect your content and delivery to build and evolve over time.

3. Get going!

Building Freshness requires a leap outside your comfort zone. There's more on how to manage that in Part 5 on Fearlessness. Keep in mind that through Freshness you can get to the hearts of your audience. By getting to the hearts of your audience, you can leave them with a powerful, memorable message.

To help you develop fresh public speaking experiences, I have developed the 'RULE' of Freshness – make sure any Freshness technique you develop is:

R – Relevant to your message and therefore relevant to the audience's reason for being there. You're not just 'doing an ice-breaker' or 'opening with a joke,' which can often be the appealing icing on a very dull-tasting cake. Instead, add colour and texture to the parts of your talk that you want your audience to remember.

U – Unique: This is achieved by doing something unforgettable in your talk. You could be unique in the emotion you use, the story you tell, the way you use your room layout, or in a host of other ways that we'll look into in this chapter. The moments that are most unforgettable for an audience often involve the most courage. Be bold – bolder than your fear tells you is acceptable.

L – Learning-focused: Remember that you are speaking to give information or inspiration, rather than to receive acclaim from your audience. Freshness should enhance, rather than detract, from learning and should give the audience the feeling of having learned something new.

E- Engaging: Finally, Freshness should encourage your audience to engage their own creativity and imagination – whether it's engaging physically or mentally. If they're not engaged, it's like a play with no audience. If they are engaged, they will take in and remember more of your message.

This section gives you a wealth of different ideas for upping the Freshness of your performance. But, as with any part of this book, it's up to you to pick the techniques that are most powerful and authentic for you to add to your Ingredients List (p. 241).

Chapter

6

Wonderful words and vibrant visuals

There are endless ways to add that memorable spark of Freshness to your public speaking. In this chapter, we'll investigate the different visual and verbal tools that are at your disposal. Think creatively about how to use each in a way that's Relevant, Unique, Learning-focused and Engaging for your audience.

Wonderful Words

No speaker can get away with avoiding words, so chose your words wisely. They could mean the difference between an 'OK' and a mind-blowing public speaking experience. Let's start with the ten main verbal techniques to deliver your content in an interesting and memorable way.

Consider your audience as having two types of information needs: Left Brain needs, or rational, fact-driven needs and Right Brain needs, or emotion-driven needs. This is more or less how the brain works according to neuroscientists, although it's a myth that people are either 'Left Brainers' or 'Right Brainers' as much pop-psychology suggests – we all use both sides of our brain. Still, different verbal tools are useful to tickle different sides of the brain. Usually a powerful speaker will appeal to both sides of the brain. Choose the most appropriate combination of these tools for your message.

1. Powerful Quote

For example:

'As Einstein said, "Imagination is more important than knowledge". In this talk, I'm going to challenge you. You won't just be listening and take notes, but you'll be cranking up that rusty imagination.'

Used for: Conjuring inspiration (for the Right Brain) and adding legitimacy to your point because someone important agrees with you – *if Einstein said it, it must be true* (for the Left Brain).

Powerful quotes work well at the beginning and end of speeches and are a safe verbal tool to use if you're a nervous speaker. Often quotes are a low-risk method for bringing humour into a speech – quotes from Mark Twain and Oscar Wilde are a good starting point. Create a collection of quotes that fit with your message. Even if you don't use them in the talk, they might be useful if you have a question and answer session afterwards.

2. Famous example

For example:

'Sometimes something happens in life that puts everything else in perspective. When 27-year-old Aron Ralston set of into the wilderness in Utah, he had no idea that he'd arrive home six days later, having escaped from underneath a boulder by amputating his own arm.'

Used for: Inspiration – *wow, he did that* (for the Right Brain) and providing evidence – *If Ralston could do something so brave, it must be logically possible* (for the Left Brain).

Famous examples are brief ways of adding legitimacy to your argument, whilst also giving a clear experience for the audience to remember afterwards. If you are telling the whole story, though, make sure that it is information new to the audience. Aron Ralton's story was made into the film *127 Hours*, so telling the whole story to an audience who have seen the movie wouldn't be appropriate.

3. Storytelling

For example:

'On my twelfth birthday, something happened that changed my life. I was never an aggressive boy. I never fought with my brother and I never cut worms in two. But that day, when a man pushed my mother to the ground and ran off with her bag, I was left with a choice: help her up, or run after the thief.'

Used for: Evoking emotions to tickle the Right Brain.

Use personal stories where it's useful for the audience to build their connection with you as a speaker and use stories from the public domain when you'd prefer attention to be on your key messages. Storytelling works best when you back it up with great intonation, brave gaps and an emotional connection to the story's message. Ensure Relevance by always linking your story to the purpose of your talk.

What's my story?

Whether you want to touch a single audience as a one-off, or many audiences as a professional speaker, finding 'your story' will help you connect to your audience in a memorable and authentic fashion. Your story is the reason why you're qualified to comment on a subject and usually involves an experience that you've gone through that changed your perspective. You can find your story in even the most mundane of situations:

'On my way to work one morning I noticed a young blackbird dancing about in the trees above me. That evening I came home and found it on the ground – a lifeless pile of feathers. That one moment got me thinking of how precious life is . . .'

Inspirational speakers use *their* story to add authenticity to their message. If you can deliver your story in a way that's vulnerable and emotional, your performance will carry more power.

4. Analogy/metaphor

For example:

'When one crab tries to climb out of a bucket filled with crabs, the others pull him back in. In order to grow, we need to support others in their attempts to change.'

Used for: Bringing the topic alive (Right Brain).

A metaphor is a way of understanding one concept by relating it to another. Analogies are extended metaphors. Both can be used extensively in public speaking to create insightful ways of expressing yourself, to get the audience's brains ticking and to help them remember your point. Next time this audience sees a crab in the supermarket, they'll remember the bucket of crabs metaphor and its message.

5. Powerful Three

For example:

'I came. [1] I saw. [2] I conquered. [3].'

Or:

'There are three things I want you to take from this evening: information, inspiration and perspiration.'

Used for: Creating emphasis and emotion (Right Brain).

Powerful threes create a steady rhythm in speaking that make you sound like a pro. They can be used in conjunction with gaps to signal key messages, or they can be used in the general body of your content to create a rhythm that feels good to the audience.

6. Strong fact

For example:

'Of the 60,000 thoughts we have every day, 95 per cent of them are the same as yesterday. And 95 per cent of them are the same as tomorrow.'

Used for: Building evidence (Left Brain).

Pepper your speech with facts, especially if you have an audience teaming with pragmatists. A strong fact is in some way dramatic and is easy to deliver. Try to spit out a complicated fact like '35 per cent of people in our sample of women thought that they were more than likely to act differently next time if given support by one or more trained specialists' and your audience will be left confused.

Strong facts hit a message more effectively than a pithy statement. Compare the statement 'We all know things are getting more expensive', with a fact like, 'In the past ten years, consumer goods increased in price by 30 per cent.' Facts add to your credibility as a speaker. Remember to research your facts well, so that if someone questions you, you're able to give them your source.

7. Evocative image

For example:

'Picture this: you're walking home alone on a windy autumn evening. A streetlight flickers hopelessly above you. As you turn the corner, you slip on a pile of wet leaves and just manage to catch yourself on some railings. But – rip – you've torn your favourite coat.'

Used for: Getting the audience to visualise and connect with you. Adding emotion and drama (Right Brain).

To create an evocative image, think like a novelist. A good author might not write, 'Jane got out of the car', but she might write, 'Jane slid her long legs out of the red sports car'. By adding colour and detail to your performance you give the audience a visual image, something to latch onto. The benefit of speaking versus the written word is that you can even evoke sound, smell, texture and taste through the words and sound effects you use – like the sounding out of the *rip* of clothing in this example.

8. Humour/telling jokes

For example:

'I'd like to begin by thanking you all for being here today. I'd like to offer my particular thanks to those of you who knew I'd be speaking – it's very touching that you still decided to come.'

Used for: Entertaining and building rapport (Right Brain).

Many nervous speakers feel that should probably 'start with a joke' to warm up the audience up. Before you use humour, refer back to our RULE of Freshness and ask yourself – how relevant is your humour to what you're trying to achieve? Is your joke a triumphant trumpet signalling that what's coming is a fast-paced, witty speech? Is it a funny insight that frames your perspective on the topic? Both of these would be excellent uses of humour.

Or is it an attempt to get your audience to listen for 20 seconds between the real, boring part of your speech starts? They say, 'once you've made an audience laugh, you've won them over', but this is only assuming you continue to engage your audience rather than bore them.

Another important element to humour is to develop your own style. We imagine that the audience will *only* like us if we're funny and we desperately want to be liked, so shouldn't we tell a joke? Not necessarily. If the traditional idea of funny doesn't work for you, find your own brand of funny.

What if... I'm not funny?

Expert tip: John Hotowka

Professional speaker John Hotowka mixes his own brand of humour with magic to create an entertaining experience for his audiences:

'If you're worried about being funny, you're on the wrong track,' he says. *'Trying* to be funny doesn't work, because the audience can tell a mile off if you're not being authentic. Focus on being entertaining instead as the purpose of your talk is much more important than getting your audience to laugh. A drama on TV isn't necessarily funny, but it can still be entertaining.

'If you want to use humour, "go ugly early" by testing your material out on a smaller audience. A lot of comedians do this before their tour, to see how well their material works in a low-risk environment.

'If you're used to raising a laugh, but your audience don't seem to be responding, don't worry. Just let it go, be authentic and polite and keep talking.'

9. Anchor word or phrase

For example:

'We're brought together by passion *and* authenticity. *The* passion *for helping people and the desire to do this in an* authentic *way . . . That's why I'm* passionate *about helping these businesses to grow . . . I work with the most* passionate, authentic *young graduates... Time and again we see it's* authenticity *that matters.'*

Used for: Adding credibility to your concepts (Left Brain). Building resonance or inspiration (Right Brain).

Anchor words are a series of words or phrases that you return to many times over the course of a talk. They give your key message time to come to the boil. Any message you deliver to an audience will be new to them even if you've delivered it a thousand times. They will need to absorb your words and ideas gently over time before feeling convinced. Hearing the same anchor words running throughout your talk, your audience will latch onto your key message more effectively than if you use many different words to describe the same concepts.

Scatter your anchor words across your talk, each time using them in different contexts and situations, or approaching them from a different perspective, so that each anchor phrase builds on your picture – important for the Learning part of the RULE of Freshness. Avoid anchors that are in the style of American documentaries, where content and facts are typically repeated a number of times during the programme. Your audience are no doubt intelligent people – so only repeat phrases and facts if it's really needed.

By creating an 'anchor', you show off your talent as a speaker and you increase the chance that your audience remember your message.

10. Song or poem

For example:

'As Bob Dylan sang in "Blowing in the Wind", "How many times can a man turn his head, and pretend that he just doesn't see?" Today it seems that we have been turning our heads away from a crucial problem in our world – the population crisis.'

Songs and poems can be a lively way to relate to your audience and they can also be deeply profound. If you're looking for the emotional touch, but aren't a poetic or emotional sort, poems are a great tool. They're often used at funerals, weddings and other family occasions, where someone else's words perfectly capture the mood of the moment.

If you're speaking to a business group, songs and poems can be risky. Take care to judge carefully whether your audience would accept a sincere poem or a playful song without feeling uncomfortable.

> Practise creating Wonderful Words for your next speech by using the Wonderful Words Bingo on p. 245.

Vibrant Visuals

Words alone can be very powerful, but visual aids add something extra for the memory to latch onto. Let's turn to the different visuals at your disposal and how you might use them in the freshest way possible.

PowerPoint

I'll start off by tackling the elephant that stands at the front of most public speaking rooms – the PowerPoint presentation. The first thing to do is to notice is the typical reflex – 'I'm due to give information to an audience, so where's my laptop?' – and question it.

Do your audience *really* need another presentation?

Although many speakers use PowerPoint to make them seem professional, you can seem more competent and refreshing as a speaker if you don't use it. I tend to avoid PowerPoint, especially when I'm running a small group workshop:

. . . because it makes people switch off.

. . . because the audience suspect this presentation has been used for various other audiences and so it's not personal to their needs.

. . . because it evokes the dynamic of a cinema – 'Here's a coloured screen, all I need to do is watch, because it doesn't interact with me.'

Using PowerPoint is a personal choice you should make based on your empathetic understanding of your audience's needs. Generally if you're speaking to a large audience or have a technical or precise message, using PowerPoint has a number of benefits. To make a powerful PowerPoint presentation, avoid the following four common crimes.

PowerPoint Crime 1: 'The desert'

The desert is page after page of dry bullet points on your slides. This is a trap speakers often fall into when they have a lot of information to convey and not much time to prepare. Whilst it's tempting to offer the audience something other than you to stare at blankly whilst you talk, this is a passive way of delivering information, which is likely to make your audience remember less of your message.

Instead, choose the points that are most important and give the details in your handouts. Populate your desert by choosing full-size, striking images, diagrams and provocative facts that show your message rather than tell it. Remember that you are the speaker, not your slides. PowerPoint should support, but not take over, what you say.

Some speakers only use images in their presentations and tell stories around what the pictures say. This technique allows you flexibility within your talk, so even if you forget your place, nobody will know.

What if . . . my subject's boring?

Expert tip: Amanda Bouch

If you think you'll be boring, you probably will be, says leadership facilitator and coach Amanda Bouch. But if you give yourself permission, you can present even the driest topic in a fresh way. Here are her top tips:

- Find the underlying principle of your topic that's interesting. Usually it's the human side of the subject that is interesting, not the straight facts.

- Focus on anecdotes and storytelling that bring your message to life.

- Present data as visually as possible by using diagrams and pictures rather than reams of numbers.

- If you do decide to use PowerPoint, limit your slides to a maximum of one per minute. Your slides shouldn't repeat what you're saying.

'There are so many terrible presentations out there', says Amanda, 'that by thinking through your message and making it more human and visual, you can really distinguish yourself as a good speaker'.

PowerPoint Crime 2: 'Panic at the disco'

'Panic at the disco' slides are filled with too many contrasting colours and animated movements. They are often designed by frustrated creatives, who would be better off taking their Picasso palette to a blank canvas than a presentation.

Although you might think your clicky, flashy, wavy features look good, the standard audiences expect these days is remarkably high and an amateur PowerPoint will stick out. Either get a professional to design an animation for you, or keep movement on slides to a minimum. If you're looking for something different, video clips are easily sourced from the internet and have become a regular part of what an audience likes and expects from a presentation.

Next, make sure your chosen colour scheme will be readable on screen. Remember that images projected onto a screen come out lighter, so background and foreground colours should be high in contrast. Print your slides in black and white to check. Avoid too many different colours, shapes and sizes of text if you are including words.

PowerPoint Crime 3: 'Overload'

'Overload' slides are where a speaker proudly presents 'Here's everything I know on a page.' Overload can come from too much writing or an over-complex diagram.

Remember:

1. It doesn't cost anything to put in extra slides.
2. You only have one mouth, so you can only talk about one message at a time. Break down your message into bite-sized chunks that appear in stages on the screen.

Anything less than 24-point font is unreadable to an audience, so if your words don't fit on the screen at that size or larger, that's a message to you to cut back on the number of words in each slide. If you really want to keep the Freshness, resolve to keep your slides to a ten-word maximum.

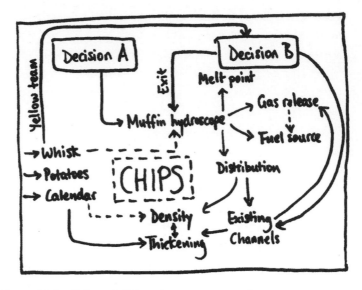

PowerPoint Crime 4: 'My notes, on a screen'

We've developed a social myth that an audience will think you a better speaker if you don't have any notes. This may hold true for professional speakers who deliver the same speech hundreds of times. But the effect of this myth on amateurs is that instead of holding notes in our hands, we put them all up on a projector screen instead. If you don't know your content and need to read from your PowerPoint presentation, either prepare more or keep your notes with you.

We've all seen speakers shift to the next slide and say, 'I wonder what I wanted to say next' or 'Oops, let's see what's on the next slide.' If your presentation is too long or complicated to remember, get a simpler, more logical structure (see Chapter 8) or print your slides.

Flipchart

A flipchart is a great, versatile visual aid that works well for groups of up to 40 people (sometimes more). I often use a flipchart to draw cartoons and diagrams for my audiences and find it much more human and authentic than PowerPoint. Even if you can't draw, think of all of the fresh uses a blank sheet of paper might have for your audience: it could be a treasure map of instructions, an entertaining diagram, a quote, a game of hangman and so on. And because you are building it together it becomes a useful and memorable visual prompt.

With a bit of time spent thinking about your audience's needs and the unique parts of your message, you can create some innovative ways to use your flipchart.

As you do that, make sure you avoid these three flipchart foes:

1. *'I'm sorry, does that say "Mother" or "Monster"?'*

    If your writing looks like a spider's run across the page, or you can't spell 'Toffee', let alone spell for toffee, then think twice before using a flipchart. As an alternative, either pre-prepare your flipchart, or invite a neat writer from the audience to take notes. Even if your writing's not bad stick to block capitals, so that your audience can clearly see your writing from a distance.

2. *'Whoops, the pen's run out'*

    There's nothing that kills the Freshness of a quick brain-storm like checking one, two, three, four pens to find one that still has ink in it. If you use a flipchart regularly, bring your own marker pens with you and test them before you start. Likewise, check there's enough paper left in the pad for your whole session.

3. *'Nice bum, shame about the face'*

    It's often useful to have one speaker talking to the audience and another taking notes on a flipchart. However, you may need to manage a group discussion and write at the same time. If this happens, avoid blocking the writing by stand-ing directly in front of your flipchart, bum sticking out at the audience. Instead, write from the side slightly, so that every-one can see what you're writing as you're writing it. This keeps the audience focused on the task and allows you in turn to collect more answers as you need them.

> **Top tip**
>
> *Hidden handwriting*
>
> If you write some notes in light pencil on a flipchart, your audience won't be able to see them. Whilst you're brainstorming, you can keep track of your key questions and topic areas without ever needing to look at your notes.

Professional speakers and trainers make brainstorming look easy, but there's a knack to it. To create an effective brainstorm on your flipchart:

- Write the title on the page. Top (title) or middle (spider diagram) are both good. Often speakers forget to do this and the audience can lose track of what they were brainstorming.

- Don't make anybody's idea wrong. Put everyone's point onto the flipchart during a brainstorm, or they may feel negative towards you. The dynamic of a brainstorm is inviting and investigating ideas, so they don't all have to fit with the answers you were expecting.

- Use the language of your audience. If their answer to the question is 'Orange Dog', don't write up 'Ginger Canine' – that's your language, not theirs.

- Keep on track. If a point that's made isn't relevant, it doesn't need to go on the flipchart, but you should bring the conversation back to the question in hand.

Props

There's nothing quite like a good old-fashioned prop for adding Freshness to your public speaking. Because 3D objects aren't commonly used in speaking, they often provide an unforgettable connection to your message. Make sure:

- The prop is big enough for everyone to see.
- You don't have too many props causing clutter – less is more.
- Your prop is relevant to the topic. Does everyone see the connection between the prop and topic, or do you need to explain it?

Props can be used to link to your key messages in clever ways:

'Inside this box are three secrets that will help every one of you to live a dramatically happier life.' [Speaker shows the audience a box, the audience immediately want to see inside. Speaker pauses for effect.] 'Now... unfortunately I've forgotten the key [audience laugh] so we'll have to work out the three secrets together.'

In this example, the speaker can continually refer back to the box as a metaphor during their speech: 'Is that important enough to go inside the box?' At the end of their talk they might find the keys to open the box and finish by reading out the final three messages.

Think of symbols and metaphors relating to your message that could become props. An accountant reminding an audience of tax return deadlines might hold up a giant brown envelope; a nutritionist speaking about diet and brittle bones might bring breadsticks to snap; and a speaker emphasising the 'many hats' they wear might bring a selection of hats to change into at different points of the talk.

Handouts

In formal talks and meetings, handouts can be an effective way to complement the structure of your talk, or to go alongside your other visual aids. Use handouts when you're giving detailed information; when the audience may need to analyse or reflect on what you're saying; or when they need to write something down. Here's how to make handouts work for you:

Take one, pass it on: Avoid sending handouts round the audience during your talk. There will be too much paper rustling, you waste precious speaking time and people will look at the new, exciting handout rather than at you. For handouts that summarise your talk, allow people to collect a copy after you've finished speaking. For handouts that you're using during the session, make sure they're ready and waiting for the audience when they enter the room. Request that the audience resist the urge to flick forwards in the handouts.

'Print 6 slides to a page': Avoid the temptation to give your audience PowerPoint slide handouts after your talk. Whilst audiences think they like the comfort of receiving the slides from a great talk, they're not as useful as we all think. How many times have you actually looked at slides after you've listened to a speech? Not very often, I suspect. And even when you do look back on printed slides, how much can you understand from them? Slides for a talk tend to be irrelevant without you speaking around them, unless your slides are laden with too much information. You're much better off spending a few minutes crafting your slides into an appealing page or two of succinct notes that your audience will refer to later.

Fill in the gap: For notes that support you during your session, encourage audience members to add their own notes and insights to your diagrams, bullet points or pictures. Avoid writing everything in handouts, as your audience face the temptation of skipping to later on in your speech if they get bored. Your audience should feel that they've got something from hearing you talk that they couldn't have read in an article written by you.

Stay in touch: Be sure to include your contact details so your audience can get in touch if they want. If relevant, include the copyright details of your materials.

Innovation

What else is there that you can do to think creatively with your visuals? Ask yourself what you can do to be more Relevant, Unique, Learning-focused and Engaging. Here are a few ideas I've used in the past:

- Use different colours for different types of message: Everything about the past could be red, everything about the present orange, and everything about the future green.

- Fill the wall with colourful quotes relating to your subject. I print out humorous public speaking quotes and place them around my workshop rooms for added inspiration during breaks.

- Use your audience as a visual aid: I've worked with kids in the past, so I sometimes get audience members up on stage to *become* letters of a mnemonic, by sellotaping giant letters to their bodies. It works for adults too!

- Create a giant timeline (or other diagram) using a flipchart on a wall, which you then add to over the course of your speech.

The sky's the limit with visuals. Have fun, be bold and you'll create a little magic.

What if . . . my audience won't accept innovation?

Expert tip: David Hyner

'There's no such thing as an audience who dislike innovation', says professional speaker David Hyner, 'but sometimes speakers worry about this because they lack imagination or confidence. So many speakers stick to familiar territory and end up delivering the same boring presentation as everyone else, but it doesn't have to be that way.

'I once worked with the CEO of a large company who knew he had some difficult figures to present at his company conference. He could have given the long, serious presentation that everyone expected, but instead he came on stage to pyrotechnics and the *Mission Impossible* theme tune, abseiling through the ceiling! That presentation is still talked about to this day.

'If you're confident, your audience will accept whatever innovative techniques or explanations you throw at them.

'If you prefer a less dramatic way of innovating, look to respected professionals in your field for inspiration. I often interview top performers to gain inspiration from them about how to present my subject. Their enthusiasm and quality of thinking gives me fresh ideas and at the very least I have an interesting story to share about interviewing them.'

Chapter

7

Ingenious interactivity

Listening is tiring for audiences. The average attention span of an audience member is just 15 minutes, so if you leave the audience watching you for a long period of time, you increase the chance they'll drift off. Interaction, on the other hand, is energising. As experiential learning theorists have demonstrated, interactivity can engage an audience in your subject matter and is a powerful tool for ensuring that they receive and retain your message.

Depending on your audience size, their needs and your confidence, there are four levels of interactivity you might use with them. See which of these you can use to bring Freshness into your speaking.

Interactivity Level 1: Rhetorical Interaction

The first level of interaction is the lowest risk: involving the whole audience, without them needing to do anything physically. Rhetorical interaction is moving the audience's attention from 'What's the speaker saying?' to 'How does what the speaker's saying apply to me?' You are getting the grey cells working, meaning that you will begin to have a room of learners rather than simply listeners.

Different methods of Rhetorical Interaction

(a) Rhetorical Questions: e.g. 'How would you feel if you put yourself in my position?' or 'How does this affect your business?' or 'What would you do if you had to make a choice between the right thing and the thing that's expected of you?'

(b) Applying a fact to audience: e.g. 'More than one in three people will develop some form of cancer during their life.

That's a tough statistic, but until it affects your life, cancer is a distant difficulty. Take a look at the neighbour either side of you and ask yourself, "Which one of us will it be?" Now how distant does cancer feel?'

(c) Stimulating memory recall: e.g. 'Many of us have fond memories of close, personal time with Sophie during her life,' [signals audience to recall a personal time spent with Sophie] or 'We all remember our first day at school . . .' [signals audience to recall their first day at school]

What Rhetorical Interaction is good for

Rhetorical Interaction is great when you don't have the time, physical space or resources available to do a more in-depth interactive exercise. Some key moments when you might use rhetorical interaction include:

- A 60-second introduction to yourself or your topic.

- A speech format where it's not expected for you to interact with the audience. Perhaps the audience is too big, perhaps the occasion is too formal, or perhaps you are being videoed with no microphones for the audience.

- During impromptu speaking. Rather than following your instinct to only talk about yourself, turn your topic onto your audience. Even if this is unrehearsed, it will show you to be a skilled speaker. Start with phrases like 'What if you . . .?', 'Imagine you were . . .' or 'Ever thought of . . .?'

Interactivity Level 2: Individual Task

An Individual Task is something you ask your audience members to do to concrete your message. Typically these are 'in the seats' exercises and can start as briefly as a 'hands up if you...' question. Here you are shifting the audience dynamic from a one-way information flow: 'I'll just listen and gather information' to a two-way interaction: 'I'm also involved in this talk.' Practical interaction increases memory recall and places the responsibility on the audience to learn.

Types of Individual Tasks

(a) Note taking: a simple form of individual interaction is encouraging your audience to take notes, or to write down your contact details. It's not the most innovative technique, but it's often neglected. Good note taking has been shown not only to be a source of information for audience members to refer back to but also to be a process to help memory recall. Encourage note taking by:

- Asking your audience to take notes: 'There'll be a lot of information in this talk, so please feel free to take notes. I'll give you a moment now to get your notebooks out.'
- Reiterating key points: 'And this is a point you'll want to note down.'
- Allowing the audience time to jot down key facts.

(b) Quiz: personalise your message by either getting your audience to test their knowledge on a subject (e.g. a right/wrong answer quiz) or testing their attitude towards it (e.g. a personality questionnaire). Quizzes often add a lively and competitive feeling to a room. After you've finished the quiz, bring the learning from it back to the whole room by getting audience members to share their answers. You can do this by a show of hands or by asking individuals for their answer.

If you're feeling bold, jazz up a quiz into a lively game by getting audience members to 'vote with their feet' and move to the part of the room that represents their answer – 'If you agree, head to the left of the room, if you disagree, head to the right of the room'.

(c) Individual exercise: go deeper with your audience by getting them to put your information into practice. You could ask your audience to write down their answers to a series of questions, complete a diagram, draw something, or any number of other possibilities. Exercises are important where you have a strong learning message and would like to test the audience's ideas or abilities whilst you're in the same room. Exercises are often, but not necessarily, supported by handouts.

Don't forget the RULE of Freshness – any exercise you create should not only be Relevant, Learning-focused and Engaging, but also Unique. Think creatively to see how you can avoid the cliché exercise and also meet the audience's needs.

(d) Question and Answers: this is the most common interaction in large audiences. It is your choice as to whether to accept questions throughout your talk, or whether you'd like to focus on them at the end. For many speakers, the idea of a Q&A is the most nerve-wracking part of a speech or presentation. Don't worry, you're not expected to know all the answers. (See the section on audience types on p. 89. for more on how to handle questions.)

Note that question and answers sessions often only involve those who are asking the question and as such can be boring for those who have already decided they don't want to ask a question. To engage more of your audience in a Q&A, you could ask 'hands up' questions, e.g. 'How many of you have had a near death experience?', 'How many of you know someone who has?', 'How many of you would consider yourselves religious?'

(e) Stand up, sit down: a favourite innovative individual task of mine uses individuals in the audience as a visual aid. Choose statistics that are key to your message and use your audience to *be* those statistics:

'Imagine that all of us in this room represent the global population. Can I ask this half of the room [gesture to 50 per cent of the audience] *to stand up please. All of those standing together own just 1 per cent of the world's wealth.*

'Now I'd like this group to stand up [gesture to about 30 per cent of the audience] *– you own about 6 per cent of the world's wealth.*

'Now may I ask the rest of you to stand up, apart from you [gesture to a small cluster of people representing 1 per cent of the audience] *– you together own about half of the world's wealth.*

'And now, let's have the final people in the room standing. These [two or three] *individuals – just them on their own –*

own 43 per cent of the world's wealth. How does that make the rest of you feel?'

You could also combine this interaction with visual aids. In this example, you might illustrate each group you refer to with an image on a PowerPoint slide, or you could 'give a gift' to each group, the first group getting a loaf of bread to share with each other and the last group getting your car keys.

What Individual Tasks are good for

Individual Tasks are usually used where you have a large number of people but your room layout prohibits them from interacting well with each other, such as when the layout is Theatre style (see p. 78). Here, the audience don't expect to interact with each other, so communication channels are between the speaker and individual audience members, rather than within the audience. Scenarios where this might be the case include:

- Academic lectures where you typically find fixed seating. A lecture with no interaction makes it easy for the audience to fall asleep.
- Groups or workshops when there isn't time for audience members to work together.
- Large audiences of an almost limitless size.

Good individual interaction engages all of the audience with the task. To make that happen, don't be afraid to make one or more requests for the audience to get involved. Stick to your requests with confidence and you'll soon have everyone participating.

Interactivity Level 3: Information Sharing

The third level of audience interaction is between members of the audience as well as with you. A century of research has shown that collaboration between learners improves the amount of information they recall.

When you engage in Information Sharing activities, your role evolves into one of a facilitator, rather than just a public speaker. This is a useful role for you to play because:

- Together you have more information than just you alone.
- It takes the pressure off you to know all the answers.
- Most people love to talk! If you give your audience a chance to hear their own voice, they're more likely to leave thinking, 'Wow, that was a really great talk.'

Types of Information Sharing

(a) Pair Share: some audiences will need warming up to interaction, such as if you're faced with a room of Snowmen (see p. 94). The Pair Share is a great way to encourage sharing in a way that feels low risk to audience members. Simply ask the audience to discuss a question in pairs, then ask volunteers to share what they've learned with the whole room. This method is effective when wrapping up the key messages of your session, e.g. 'Tell your partner the main thing you want to do differently when you've left this room'. Individuals may not want to share such information with the whole room, but sharing with a partner may feel more comfortable.

(b) The Snowball: as an extension of the Pair Share, you can use a Snowball to debate an idea through the whole room. This works well if you'd like to develop consensus in an audience containing many diverse opinions:

1. After a Pair Share, get the pairs to bundle together with another pair and discuss a question, e.g. 'What is the future for our organisation?' The group of four should come to a consensus.

2. Next, get each group of four to combine with another group of four who have a different opinion and discuss the question again. Once again, consensus should be reached.

3. You can continue doing further rounds for as long as it takes to achieve consensus within the whole audience. Usually two or three rounds are enough, before discussions begin to get repetitive.

4. Bring the discussion back to the whole room and ask each group to comment about the consensus that was reached.

(c) Facilitated discussion: to facilitate a discussion is to help your audience express thoughts and ideas relating to your topic. Your role is no longer to provide information, but to help others to express their ideas; to challenge those ideas and to draw themes from the group that further your key messages. By involving the audience in a form of discussion, they will more effectively remember your message and will be able to apply that information in different settings afterwards.

Some rules of good facilitation:

1. Agree your role with the audience: explain that your role will not be to give your opinion, but to facilitate the discussion. This is particularly important in discussions that might become personal or emotional. If your authority is agreed with the audience, you will have their support if, for example, you need to stop a thread of discussion that is counterproductive.

2. Start with the right question: the question framing your discussion should be well thought through. Test your question with a few friends or colleagues by brainstorming the answers they would give. Does your question lead the discussion in the right direction?

3. Manage the discussion:

   ● Use Socratic Questioning (see below): this encourages audience members to develop a deeper understanding of arguments and ideas. This is useful for all facilitators as they try to open up the audience to new ways of looking at the topic.

   ● Trim the waffle: if an audience member is taking up too much airtime or bringing little benefit, take firm control. Cut in at a pause and thank them for their input; ask them to be brief with their answers; or set the expectation in advance that everyone should be brief and focused with their input.

Socratic Questioning

There are six types of Socratic Question that are helpful to master as a facilitator:

1 'Tell me more' Questions

   Used to open up a discussion, to encourage more details about a thought process, or to clarify its relevance.

   – 'What do you think about this?'

   – 'What does that mean?'

   – 'Say more?'

   – 'How does that relate to my question?'

2 Foundation-rocking Questions

   Probing questions that challenge participants' assumptions of their argument.

   – 'Is that always true?'

   – 'When else is what you're saying true?' 'When is it not true?'

   – 'What assumptions are you making?'

3 Reasoning Questions

   Testing the strength of the argument given.

   – 'What evidence do you have to support that argument?'

   – 'How do you know that's true?'

   – 'What do you think causes that?'

4 Alternative Perspective Questions

   Expanding the range of possible solutions in a group.

   – 'What's another way of looking at that?'

   – 'How would this look from a child's/manager's/outsider's perspective?'

   – 'What's the counter-argument?'

5 Consequences Questions

Analysing the implications of a line of reasoning.

– 'What would happen if . . .?'

– 'Why is that important?'

– 'How could we use this to help us . . .?'

6 Question the Question

Allowing the audience to evaluate the relevance of the discussion to them.

– 'Why do you think I'm asking this question?'

– 'How relevant is this discussion to your life?'

– 'What's important about this question?'

Historically, Socrates enjoyed using questions to delve into his audience's argument and then show them why their thinking was wrong. Facilitators tend not to judge the outcome of a discussion, but aim to deepen the learning of participants. The exception is in a teaching environment, where you might be looking to get a specific conclusion to the discussion.

- Involve all members of the audience: spread the discussion to members of the group who aren't participating fully. Encourage those quieter audience members by asking them open questions such as 'What do you think?' rather than closed questions such as 'Do you agree?' Assume that everyone has useful input to give.

4. Manage yourself: the way a facilitator behaves will be reflected in how the group behaves. So, if you are anxious or overly curt with facilitation, the level of tension will increase in the group and you may find a heated discussion developing. If you stay calm, so will the general atmosphere within your audience, even if one or two members of the group find the topic emotional.

(d) Group tasks: these involve splitting your audience into sub-groups. In a group task, individuals share information within a group of three to six and answer questions or complete an activity together. Some group tasks include:

- Discussing a question together and brainstorming the answers on flipchart.

- Group members sharing opinions on the subject in hand.

- Completing a quiz together, in competition with other groups.

Group challenges are a fantastic way to spread the learning within the room and to help your audience interact more closely with the subject matter. They are particularly effective when you have audience members seated around tables, or with plenty of room to move chairs into small circles.

What Information Sharing interactions are good for

Information sharing is most relevant when you'd like your audience to interact with your topic and apply their own thinking to it. It's also a useful and productive way to fill time in a speaking schedule, because one exercise could last anything from a couple of minutes to a number of hours. Information Sharing works best in a small to medium-sized group, but it can also work well in larger groups if you have enough:

- Space to move: for example, a lecture theatre is a more difficult format for Information Sharing within the audience, because of fixed seating.

- Time for people to discuss: remember that interactive discussions often take longer than you think.

Some conference facilities are now offering live Twitter 'back-chanelling' screens to help larger audiences interact with their speaker. This is a time-saving and modern way to engage in discussion with your audience and it also allows you to interact with an audience who may not even be in your room, through live streaming. But make sure you can switch off the Twitter stream if it becomes distracting. Cliff Atkinson has written a book, *The Backchannel*, explaining how to duck the dangers of social media's new influence in public speaking.

Information Sharing interactions can be energising and exciting, but they can also be difficult to predict or manage. Don't enter this kind of interaction if you have a short time-frame. For highly factual messages where an expert is imparting information (such as a legal briefing), or highly personal messages where your story doesn't need to be commented on (such as a speech or toast), information-sharing activities are unlikely to be relevant.

Interaction Level 4: Learning by Doing

This final level of audience interaction is a step onwards from Information Sharing. Now you're looking to immerse your audience in a journey where they're learning from a practical situation you go through together.

Types of Learning by Doing activities

(a) Experiential games and simulations: a step on from a group challenge is to design a game or simulation in which audience members play a role in an activity as if it were real life. If a game sounds too flippant or unprofessional to be worthwhile, keep in mind that research shows they not only increase interest in your topic, but also increase the learning a participant retains.

To gain confidence in the effectiveness of game playing, you'd greatly benefit from speaking to young people at least once in your career. Young people are quite happy to show when they're bored, in a way that we learn to hide later in life. Bring out a game and you'll see not only how much they enjoy it but also how powerful this format is for creating Relevant, Unique, Learning-focused and Engaging experiences.

A wonderful training organisation, Future Foundations, uses all sorts of interactive games for groups of 20 to 100 young people to teach their key messages. They have young people steering one another with blindfolds on (message: responsibility and choice); individuals falling backwards from a height to be caught by a team (message: going beyond your fears); and races to get your team across a 'toxic swamp' (message: planning and working as a team). They are then debriefed about the game and learning messages are shared within the group.

Whenever I have transferred games into an adult learning context, no matter how 'formal' the situation, they have gone down well, so long as I emphasise the Relevance of the game to the topic. Sometimes adults even become more competitive than the kids! Games are at their most effective when participants are debriefed skilfully, through good facilitation.

Some of the experiential games and simulations I've used include:

- 'Um Game' groups competing against each other (see the Um Game p. 243) (message: become aware of your speaking habits).

- Putting together a jigsaw puzzle (great for 'piecing together the big picture' messages).

- Building a bridge, straw tower, paper animal or collage (used for all sorts of messages: time management, resource management, team working, etc).

There's no limit with experiential games. Do bear in mind that such exercises can take some time to prepare, but your audience will appreciate the effort you put in.

(b) Practice: some messages are based around practical skills that are best cemented into the minds of your audience by practice and feedback. For example, the most powerful and memorable thing I can do for my public speaking students is to encourage them to get up in front of an audience and speak. By going through the motions in a safe environment, they are able to learn lessons that are far deeper than any other form of speaking. If you have a lot of time, a small

audience and a skills-focused message to deliver, practice is the most powerful and practical technique I can think of.

You can make practice most effective by:

- Making sure the practice simulation is as relevant as possible, by using real-life examples that relate to the audience.

- Giving feedback on each person's performance. If you have too many participants to do this yourself, get the audience to give each other feedback.

- Linking practice to the learning content that you've offered the audience earlier in your talk.

What Learning by Doing interactions are good for

Learning by Doing is the most interactive set of tools. These techniques are relevant in learning environments like workshops and conferences, more so than formal speeches. To run a good Learning by Doing exercise, be sure to:

- Allow plenty of time and physical space for the interaction.

- Practise well before you do your exercise for the first time, so that you're aware of what questions will be in the minds of your audience.

- Expect a few members of the audience to need persuasion to get fully involved in the exercise. Have it clear in your mind why you are doing the task and what benefit participants will get from it.

- Keep a back-up activity in mind if your exercise is new, in case it doesn't work. Information Sharing interactions are often good to have as back-up.

- End by bringing the whole group back together to summarise the key things you learned.

Freshness workout

☐ **Get creative by deciding to add innovation to your next public speaking assignment.** Become passionate about creating innovative experiences for your audience.

☐ **Pick three ways to make your visuals more vibrant.** Try jazzing up your traditional PowerPoint, or losing it all together. Experiment with props, a flipchart and other innovative visual aids.

☐ **Make your words more wonderful by choosing three techniques to spice up your delivery.** Try a powerful quote, a poem, humour or an evocative image to make your message more memorable. Be bold with your choice.

☐ **Boost the interactivity of your speaking.** Involve your audience more effectively by cranking up the amount of interaction you use in your next public speaking assignment.

☐ **Enjoy yourself.** Freshness is all about creating an engaging experience for your audience, so have fun when you're thinking of new ideas. Take yourself to a new environment to gain inspiration.

Part

4

If you can't write your message in a sentence,
you can't say it in an hour.

Dianna Booher

Lucy Longtalk glanced at her audience and frowned. 'Why are they fidgeting so much?' she asked herself.

They had been so enthusiastic when she'd first started talking. Everyone had questions and there was even a moment where the whole group had clapped something she'd said. But now, 55 minutes later, they had glazed looks on their faces and a couple of them were even checking their phones as she was speaking.

'It's like a completely different audience,' Lucy thought, 'What's gone wrong?'

Balance

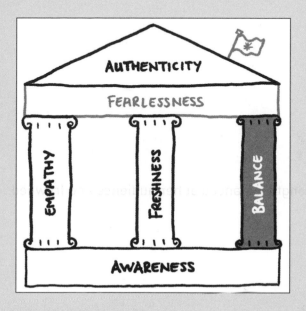

So many otherwise brilliant public speakers are tripped up by not getting the balance right. They talk for too long. They put too much emphasis on one area to the detriment of the rest of their talk. They try and fit too much in. So Part 4 is all about getting the balance right.

Balance brings order and power to your speaking. It is all about organising your information so that it is at the very least comprehensible and at best a powerful way to influence your audience.

What is perfect Balance?

- Picking content that contains the right amount of the right type of information.
- Designing content flow that is as effective as possible for its purpose.
- Ordering the flow of information to add drama so that the audience leave with your key points in their minds.
- Creating compelling structures that help you – and your audience – to remember your words.

As with many things in life, get your planning right and the rest will fall beautifully into place. So it is with public speaking. Planning the structure of your talk will make it brilliant.

Public speaking without a strong structure is like building a skyscraper out of jelly. If the form of your talk is slipping and wobbling about in front of you as you speak, if you're taking on-the-spot decisions about what information to put where, you will not construct the most effective message and will miss the opportunity of delivering it to your audience.

Structure is not:

- **A set of shackles:** Once you have devised your structure, it is not something that you have to stick to obsessively throughout your talk. As I mentioned earlier, it is often the moments when we go off-piste (either through a mistake, or through our own passion) when we seem more human and more likeable as a speaker. As you design your structure, keep that freedom in the back of your mind.

- **Personality outsourcing:** No matter how good your structure is, you'll still need to use your Awareness, Empathy and Freshness qualities to have an impact.

- **A formula:** Every talk has a slightly different purpose, so there is no single 'winning formula' for your structure. If there were, audiences would quickly become bored of it and crave something innovative. Be creative with balance and find out what works for you, to keep your audience engaged and inspired.

Structure *is*:

- **Your personal assistant:** Structure is a way of organising your thoughts before you speak, so that you don't have to do too much thinking and decision-making when you're on stage.

- **Your rock:** Structure is a firm, centred base for you to rely on, so that you can innovate or improvise and still come back to your central points.

- **Your power:** By establishing your key moments in advance of speaking, you no longer need to conjure inspiration as you're speaking – you're simply following a plan in which you have confidence. When the decision's already been made internally, you stand the best chance of putting your full force behind a powerful moment.

How do you develop Balanced Structure?

We'll look at three elements of structure that help you to create balance:

1. **Balanced Flow**: The big picture journey of your talk.
2. **Balanced Plot**: How you will organise your content into a compelling story.
3. **Balanced Content**: What you will say and when.

Chapter

8

The balancing act of structure

Balanced Flow

First, let's create a high-level map of your talk. Without a structured flow, the message to your audience is 'Here's a load of information . . . you figure it out!'

The most straightforward and common speaking flow is the classic 'Headlines – Content – Headlines' that you can see every evening on most news programmes. It gives your audience the security of knowing roughly what your talk is about and it's a good framework for any talk. In terms of how you break this down into timed chunks it would typically look like this:

Headlines	*10% of your time*
Content	*80% of your time*
Summary/Conclusion	*10% of your time*

All too often the Summary/Conclusion is missed out in a rush to cover everything else. This is a mistake. That last 10 per cent is key to helping your audience make sense of and remember your message.

For example:

Headlines: *'Today I'm here to tell you about fire safety in your new homes. I'll be talking you through the three key points I want you to remember and then showing you a rather striking demonstration.'*

Content: *'So, let's start with the first section – how fire works. I'll start with a couple of questions for you . . .'*

Summary/Conclusion: *'To wrap up, let's recap the three main messages – which are?'*

Now that we have a basic frame, let's start to flesh it out.

Lessons from storytellers

When they write, most storytellers will map out the peaks of drama in their tale so that they can pace the action to keep their readers engaged. This is a useful exercise for us as well.

Now I'm not expecting you to start utilising amateur dramatics to liven up your talk. But you can use this idea to structure your talk. However, instead of drama, think in terms of energy.

'Energy' can mean various different types of emotion: a motivational speaker may leave his audience with the emotion of optimism – 'Yes, I can do it!', a company team leader may leave her audience with the emotion of shock – 'We really need to work harder' and an event organiser may leave his guests with the emotion of celebration – 'Wow, this is great, let's party!'

As speakers, we aim to create the most appropriate flow for our subject matter, to ensure that the audience leave the room inspired. It may look something like the flow below.

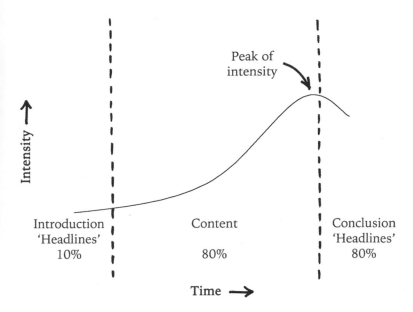

Adapted from Fretag's Pyramid

Mistakes to avoid in mapping your flow

Take care to create a flow that inspires rather than confuses. You've probably experienced a talk that just didn't seem to connect the dots, no matter how sensible the individual points seemed to be. That can happen when the speaker falls into one of the following traps.

Trap 1: A road to nowhere

Imagine you have a talk to deliver which is imparting vital information. It might be a health and safety talk, your company's new strategy or the latest sales results. These are the sort of presentations that are vulnerable to sustained low intensity.

You deliver your information relentlessly, like a road trip through an endless desert, with nothing to entertain or enliven the facts. Eventually you will get to your destination, but you'll have lost the audience's attention. They'll be staring out of the window, watching the tumbleweed, wishing they were somewhere else. And they won't remember a thing you've said.

Remember, if your audience don't sense that your talk is building towards something, you might as well be reading a shopping list to them. This is not good territory if you're hoping to influence your audience to think differently about your topic.

Imagine that same talk, but instead of dumping information on them you show them piece by piece how health and safety or strategy or sales performance contributes to a safe/successful/profitable workplace. If you could take your audience on that journey, pointing out interesting features and building excitement on the way, it would be an enjoyable, memorable and behaviour-changing experience for them. And they'd be sure to remember what you said.

Avoid Trap 1

Seek a flow that turns up the intensity as you progress.

Trap 2: The 'in your face' approach

Just as low intensity throughout will reduce the impact of your talk, so will constant high intensity. Think of how grating 'hard-hitting' adverts can be in just a short dose. Now imagine what your audience may feel if they are subjected to such intensity over 10 minutes, 20 minutes, or longer.

It can happen easily if you're desperate for your audience to agree with your message and you're unaware of how you affect your listeners. If your intensity starts high and continues at that same height for your whole talk, your audience may:

- Find it difficult to keep up with your argument.
- Feel 'spoken at' or 'bossed about'.
- Feel exhausted or panicked, as if there isn't any time for them to think.
- Subconsciously decide you are too intense for them to listen to and switch off.

Building up intensity within a room is like boiling a kettle – it takes time. That's not to say that you can't act with a burst of emotional intensity at the beginning of a talk – in fact this is often a powerful way to begin. But after this burst, don't expect your audience to be immediately 'boiling' with you, even if they've already been warmed up by another speaker, or by other circumstances.

Eddie Izzard may step on stage and have his audience laughing in five seconds and Tony Robbins may have his audience whooping and clapping within a minute, but there will still be a moment later on in their performance where the intensity peaks. During this moment, either Izzard's punchlines or Robbins' motivational empowerment have reached their crescendo *and* the audience are right there with them, enjoying every second. Without the build-up these moments are simply not powerful.

Your flow, then, should gently tease the audience towards your message, giving them the freedom to join you at the peak by choice, rather than by force.

Avoid Trap 2

Don't peak too soon. Build your intensity over time together with the audience.

Trap 3: There and back again

The final flow mistake resembles a mountain. Here, the speaker spends time setting up a story, or a major highlight of the talk, hits their peak and then continues for the same amount of time again to take the story to a conclusion. Although this structure may appeal because of its symmetry, it isn't the most powerful structure for most public speaking situations.

If you want your audience to leave remembering the powerful part of your talk, get to your peak and then finish shortly afterwards.

Consider the story of Edmund Hillary climbing to the top of his literal mountain as it might be told in a speech. Although we're interested in the minute details of his struggle *up*, we don't want the story to take us all the way back down again in detail in the final section. As far as the audience are concerned, we want Hillary to be airlifted off Everest just after he reaches the summit and then perhaps to meet him again, tucked up next to a warm fire, for a short conclusion.

If you found yourself wishing that the *Lord of the Rings* had ended shortly after Frodo and Sam destroyed the ring in Mount Doom, you wouldn't be alone. Tolkein's original ending fell into the 'There and back again' trap (appropriately enough) and left his readers wondering when they could make their excuses and leave.

A conclusion is, of course, necessary. Indeed, this is where the most inspiring speakers call their audience to action. If your call to action is close to the peak of your talk, it will have more power behind it.

Avoid Trap 3

Get to your peak and then wrap up quickly.

How to build intensity

Once you've identified where you want your peaks of intensity in your flow, it's time to add that intensity to your performance.

To build intensity, put a combination of the other public speaking skills into action. Use your Speaker's Toolkit to give a powerful delivery: use the tricks learned in Empathy to make what you're saying relevant to your audience; deliver the content with Freshness; and put your full character Fearlessly behind your performance. As you get closer to your peak of intensity, crank up the dramatic parts of your delivery to indicate to your audience that we're getting to the crux of the action.

Consider John F. Kennedy's 'Ask not what your country can do for you' speech which you can find online. He uses the following tools to build up to the peak of the speech:

- Tapping his lectern and using powerful gestures.
- Repeating key phrases like 'Let both sides' and 'a call to'.
- Increasing his volume almost to the point of shouting as he says 'I do not shrink from this responsibility – I welcome it.'
- Using shorter sentences as he wishes the drama and pace to be increased.
- Expressing himself through passionate intonation.

You can also build intensity by devising a 'plot' for your speech.

Balanced Plot: Choosing a story-line

Our flow that's structured around the news format is a useful frame, but it doesn't go nearly far enough to help most speakers, because there is a gulf of 80 per cent of the content left unaccounted for in the middle of the talk. What on earth do you do with all that time?

The next step in creating a Balanced Structure is to decide on a plot that feels right for your message. A plot is used as:

- A frame to organise your content around.
- A way of building intensity.
- A method of bringing familiarity and enjoyment to your talk by making subtle references to storytelling.

Plot conjures a sense of balance. Just as there is something satisfying about a storybook with a rounded ending, your public speaking will be more inspiring if it nourishes your audience.

Melodrama

This is a story, often personal to the speaker, that resembles the plot of so many Hollywood movies: we introduce our character and see the general state of affairs in their life. Next, something terrible happens and our main character has to struggle through adversity to end up at a climax which is higher or better than their start point.

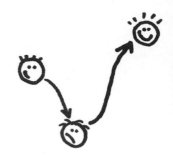

Suitable for: any occasion where you want to build emotional intensity, e.g. personal speeches, inspirational talks or when selling. A melodrama could be the whole speech, or one part of a larger structure.

Intensity Builder: *What happens in the end? Will our hero make it?*

Most inspirational speakers will have a melodrama that they use to demonstrate the journey they have been on to get to their current position. If you do it in a way that's authentic to you, a melodrama can build credibility, support your main messages and emotionally engage your audience. So, whether or not you're an inspirational speaker, you can still create a buzz of inspiration in the room by using this structure. Steve Jobs uses melodrama to wonderful effect when talking about his journey with Apple:

Start: Growing Apple from a garage enterprise into a $2 billion company.

Drama: 'And then I got fired.'

Rebuilding: Starting NeXT and Pixar, and falling in love with an amazing woman who would become my wife . . .

Peak: Returning to Apple, using the technology developed at NeXT to rebuild Apple. And having a wonderful family.

His message: None of this would have happened if I hadn't been fired from Apple.

The Tower

This structure uses different layers of information to build on the one before. The result is a compelling tower of information that supports your key message. With each layer, you gain the audience's acceptance of your argument, so that your listeners help to hold up the complete structure. When you're finished you can stand back and see the power and relevance of the argument you've constructed.

Suitable for: messages where rational reasoning is emphasised, e.g. technical messages, persuasive speeches, sales talks and academic talks.

Intensity Builder: *What's at the top of the tower?*

For example:

'We've seen today how data are collected from local and national populations [Layer 1]. But to decide whether the government's decision-making is bad or good [top layer/flag], we first need to look at how that data are analysed [Level 2] and delivered to ministers [Level 3].'

Mystery

This structure begins by setting up a question or problem. This should be something that the audience are desperate to know, but you won't tell them yet. Then, with their attention held on accessing that crucial piece of information, you take the audience

'round the houses', giving the background information that leads to the answer. This is a structure used in 'murder mystery' stories and can also be used effectively in a variety of speech settings.

Suitable for: Messages that are playful, dramatic or learning-orientated, e.g. workshops and speeches.

Intensity Builder: *Audience want to know 'What's the answer?'*

For example:

'Would you like to know how to earn £50k in a week? Well, by the end of today you will know how. But first, let's start with the basics.'

'I was standing on the edge of a building, legs wrapped in rope, staring down. My knees were shaking uncontrollably and I couldn't feel my fingers. I was about to face my lifelong fear of heights by doing a bungee jump. But would I manage it? Do you think I jumped? Let me take you back to three years earlier, when my journey into fear began.'

Ping-pong

Ping-pong is a good way to create energy in a room by looking at two sides of an argument. You can structure your 'Ping-pong game' as Side A, Side B, then conclusion and picking a winning side or, if you want to make the comparison more vivid, try bouncing between each side of the argument a number of times. Add extra oomph by using different spaces in the room to represent each side of the argument.

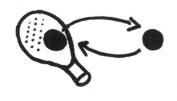

Suitable for: Messages where there are two clear sides to debate, such as moral lessons, business meetings and informational lectures. This structure also works well for pair presentations.

Intensity Builder: *Audience want to know 'Who's going to win?'*

For example:

'Should libraries be managed by the community, or by local government? Let's step into both camps to see the pluses and minuses ...'

Think about how these and other public speaking plots can create inspirational moments for your audience.

Balanced Content: Organising what to say

A mistake many speakers make is to think that organising the content of the spoken word is the same as the written word. Whilst you may naturally have a writing style that translates well into the spoken word, most written reports, documents, stories and articles have far too much information, structured in the wrong way, for public speaking.

The final step towards creating a Balanced Structure is to choose which information will – and will not – make the cut for your talk.

The Content Pie

A foolproof way of structuring your content is to order it into easy-to-remember groups of threes. I have devised the Content Pie, a tool to help you to categorise and prioritise which content you keep and which you leave. The Content Pie contains one Core message with three Themes. Each Theme has three Sections and each of the Themes has three Details. All of this is surrounded by the Crust of your Content Pie.

The Content Pie helps you to:

- Distil your ideas to the most critical ones for your audience. You only have space for 27 details, so it's a brilliant way of cutting out the waffle from your speech.
- Summarise long ideas into keywords that fit into the Pie so you can remember your content more effectively.
- Present a clearer, more memorable message: three single ideas are much more vivid than a mass of information.
- Keep an overview of your content, which allows you to balance different priorities in your talk and manage your flow.

The Content Pie creates a stable centre of gravity for your content, so that you feel confident in your material and can go on to inspire your audience.

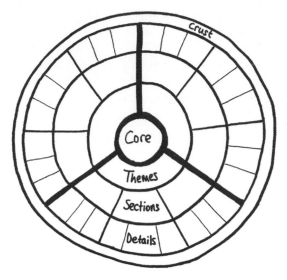

The Content Pie

Why Three?

Three is often suggested as the magic number for public speaking, yet there have been no scientific studies to confirm our preference for Magic Threes. So why group your speech into threes?

Threes are deeply embedded in our culture as easy ways to remember things. Most people share the feeling that if they have one piece of information, they can probably slot another piece of information either side to make three in total. It could be something to do with religion: Christianity has the Holy Trinity and the three Kings; Judaism has the three patriarchs; Hinduism has Brahma the Creator, Vishnu the Preserver and Shiva the Destroyer; and Buddhism has the Three Jewels, Buddha, Dharma and Sangha.

There is something satisfying and effortless about a three. And since you want to make what you say as effortless as possible for your audience to experience, threes are a good way to go.

To reorder your material into groups of threes you may need to take a new look at it. Give it a good shot as it could really benefit your message.

Still, some topics group naturally into threes and others just wont. This model is an ideal, rather than a one-size-fits-all concept. Don't worry if you have three points in one section, four in another and two points somewhere else.

The Core: The heart of your message

The guru of dramatic writing Lajos Egri said that every successful story must have a 'premise', or core message. Just as *Romeo and Juliet* held at its core the message 'great love defies even death', your speaking will be more likely to move your audience if it focuses around a single core.

A Core gives you:

- **Direction:** Everything you say can now be directed back to support your core message.

- **Simplicity:** Picking only one core means that you're not trying to do too much in your talk. If you've ever left a talk feeling confused about what the speaker was trying to say, that's probably because there was no core, or there were a number of different cores confusing the message.

- **Power:** Your core is like a sharpened chisel which will get you through the wall quicker than a blunt rock would. If every word you say chips away at your key message from different angles, you'll leave your audience buzzing with a sense of something having changed as a result of your public speaking.

How do I define my Core?

Your Core is the impact you aim to have on your audience – the change in mindset you want to create with your words. Spend time getting your core right if it's not obvious:

- What do you *really* want your audience to think, feel or know as a result of your speaking?

- What is the meaning underneath everything you're saying?

- What *movement* do you want to create in your audience?

Here are the core messages of some famous speeches:

Martin Luther King – *I Have a Dream* *– Core: Economic justice for all.*

Mahatma Gandhi – *'Quit India' Core: Insist on non-violent independence.*

Winston Churchill – *'We shall fight them on the beaches' Core: Never give up.*

As you see from these examples, your Core is not necessarily the same as your title or topic. Let's consider how I might adapt this book to deliver a speech on it. The topic is Public Speaking, which is the subject matter, but that's not my core message. The Core of the book is the premise that 'Anyone can learn to speak well in any situation', so this is the implicit or explicit focus of every chapter, section and individual line.

Core messages for rigid speech formats

If you are asked to deliver a speech at a formal occasion, the Core message may be prescribed for you. If this is the case, be sure to be aware of your Core message and keep everything you say firmly directed at it. If it's not relevant to your Core, don't say it. Here are some prescribed core messages:

Eulogy: The deceased will be fondly remembered

Prize acceptance speech: I'm grateful (e.g. ... for the help that got me here).

Birthday/anniversary speech: How wonderful the person in question is.

Introducing and thanking a headline speaker: Introducing – what a great speech this will be. Thanking – what a great speech that was.

Wedding speeches are a little flexible in their Core message. But if in doubt, use the following Cores rather than risk causing an upset:

Father of the bride speech: Welcome!

Groom speech: Thank you!

Best man speech: Wishing the couple a happy life together.

What if I have more than one Core message?

As mentioned, powerful public speaking can only have one Core message. Imagine Churchill saying, 'We shall fight them on the beaches' and then finishing his speech with, 'Oh, by the way, what I really need right now is a new pair of shoes.' If you find yourself grappling with more than one potential Core you can:

1. **Zoom out.** Find a broader Core message that encapsulates all of your important messages. Do this by working out what connects each of these themes on a high level.

   For example, back in the land of *Romeo and Juliet*, you might see Shakespeare's Core messages as 'Everything is fate', or 'Individuals matter more than society', or 'Violence is acceptable if it comes from passion'. If you try to push each of these messages as *the* central part of the story, you change the balance of *Romeo and Juliet*. It turns from being one of the world's greatest love stories into a confusing mixture of ideas. But, if you zoom out, you can see that these messages are actually Themes that support the previously mentioned Core message, 'Great love defies even death'.

2. **Do more than one speech.** If you really do have more than one Core message, it's time to divide up your speaking time.

   Look at Noam Chomsky, the linguist and political activist. His career has made him famous for research into how we learn to speak as children as well as for his views on anarchy. Unless the Core message was 'What a rich life Noam Chomsky has had', he would give one speech to talk about language and a separate one to talk on anarchy.

   So if you want to have 'Let's celebrate the major contract we just won' as one key message and 'Let's talk about redesigning our logo' as another key message, you need more than one speech or talk. The best way to arrange this is to have some physical time or another speaker in between your different Core messages, so your audience see them as different pieces of information.

Three Themes: The broad brush-strokes

Your themes are like acts in a play. They are the broad topic areas, or distinct approaches, that contribute to your Core message. If you were to have only  one Theme, your talk would risk seeming either repetitive or boring. If you have too many Themes they lose their impact as your audience won't recall what was said. Stick to the optimum Three Themes where at all possible.

Example Themes:

'Past → Present → Future' is a good standard structure for many types of talk:

George's Retirement: A touching way to celebrate George's contribution to his company might be to use the themes:

Before George (Past)

During George (Present)

After George (Future)

Malawi Appeal: A charity activist might encourage support from a group by using the themes:

The challenge of Malawi (Past)

Boreholes and schools: The project in action (Present)

A future? They need your support (Future)

Another common theme, often used in business and politics, is based around ideal situation, current situation and how to get there:

Strategy Meeting: A manager may use the following themes to rouse extra effort from within her team:

Building the Olympic Village (ideal future)

Crisis point (current situation)

Action plan (how to get there)

If your message is unique, you'll need to design your own themes.

How do I define my themes?

Taking this book as an example again we can see six themes, one per part, that support the Core premise. *Anyone can speak well in any situation* by building their: Authenticity, Awareness, Empathy, Freshness, Balance and Fearlessness. Six themes or more are fine in a book, but wouldn't necessarily translate well into public speaking. Let's have a look at some of the options that would be available to me if I were delivering a speech about this book.

Option 1: Talk about all six themes, giving each theme equal speech time.

This would be the tempting structure to use. It mirrors my message exactly, so it's just what I want to say. It's also ready to go, so I'd need less time to prepare the speech for my audience. This is often what happens with busy speakers, especially experts in their field who have previously written a report, story or article without a live audience in mind. The public speaking springing from this method of setting structure runs the risk of being neither Fresh nor Empathetic.

Six themes are likely to be too many, especially in a short speech, since we know that the audience will remember threes most effectively. The audience may leave having only a thin understanding of each of the six themes, rather than feeling really moved on a couple of key points. If I wanted to use Option 1 I would have to make reference to the six themes a number of times, to ensure they were memorable.

Option 2: Choose just one of the six themes to go into deeply and pull three themes from that.

This option basically moves one of the themes into the Core position. Rather than 'Anyone can speak well in any situation', my Core could then become something like 'Build empathy to impress an audience'. Here I could tell the audience the public speaking house framework in the introduction and then dive into

Empathy as my chosen focus area. I would still need to uncover three themes relating to Empathy to structure my content around.

Option 3: Talk about all six themes briefly, but then pick three to focus on more deeply.

This option is useful if I want to give my audience an overview on my topic, whilst also have them remember some depth of information. I could talk about either the three pillars, or the three layers.

This approach could be useful if I'm hoping to sell follow-up sessions from my talk – 'There are three more steps in this process, which I can tell you about in more detail next time.' In this option I would have to take care though. If I failed to explain my structure clearly, it may seem to the audience like I'm missing out sections, or that they are less important than the others.

Option 4: Turn the six themes into three themes

Alternatively, I could look for creative ways to make my six points into a powerful three. For example, theme one could be stories about public speaking nightmares, theme two could be presenting the public speaking house and theme three could be giving the audience a chance to practise.

Any of these options could work. Experiment with your themes until you find the ones that best represent your Core message.

What if . . . I don't have much time to prepare?

Expert tip: Paul McGee

'If you don't have time to prepare as thoroughly as this you can still give an impressive performance,' says Paul McGee, one of the UK's leading business speakers. 'The key is to find a story to tell that relates to your key message.

'You'd be surprised how many stories you have or have heard that illustrate your point in a colourful way. Say you're suddenly asked to talk about fireworks. You could ramble on about China, gunpowder, etc. Or you could tell a story about your first bonfire night and what happened to you that made it special.

'To tell a good story, use the 'three Gs':

'**Grab** their attention by using an intriguing hook. This can come from what you say and how you say it. **Give** them the content of your story to inspire or inform. And then say 'Goodbye**. Short and sweet is better for everyone than over-staying your welcome.'

Nine Sections: The meaty bits

Sections are like scenes in a play, where you begin to see the characters and topics of the play coming to life. Sections are substantial chunks of information such as stories, games and analogies. Your speech length will determine how much information goes into each.

Whilst I'd recommend using three themes where possible, your number of sections is more flexible than the number of themes. As with themes though, bear in mind that too many sections will lessen your clarity and impact.

For example:

Core: **Physics affects everything we do**

Theme: **A changing world (looking into the past)**

Sections: **The role of physics in communications**

The role of physics in product design

The role of physics in medicine

Twenty-seven Details: The nitty gritty

Now that you have your Core, Themes and Sections, the difficult work is done. Slotting in arguments to support the Section, Theme and Core should come naturally.

On this *nitty gritty* level, you're looking for the in-depth evidence that brings life to your talk. This is where we find the detailed brush-strokes that turn a rough painting into a masterpiece. By gathering your 27 Details, you will ensure your talk is based on specifics rather than waffle. You can see which section needs some more research or creative thinking to make it interesting.

An individual Detail might be:

- One of three main learning points of an exercise, game or discussion.
- A powerful fact or figure.
- A short, illustrative exercise, e.g. 'Hands up if you've been to Austria.'
- A quote, poem or metaphor.
- A powerful phrase or soundbite.

For example:

Core: **Wake up and live a healthier life**

Theme: **Theme 1: Diet**

*Section: **The Five A Day Myth***

Details:

1. **Fact: There are 13 vitamins and fruit supplies one of them – vitamin C**

2. **Question: A knob of butter on vegetables – healthy or unhealthy?**

3. **Interactive Quiz: Pick the healthiest meal: fish omelette, chicken stir-fry or liver pâté on toast**

To help you find compelling details, bring in the lessons from other parts of this book. Remember to:

- Draw from your Audience-focused Preparation to see how you can answer the burning questions your audience have.

- Provide clear, fresh and engaging evidence to support your sections and themes.

- Use details to form key moments in your talk – where you use gaps, intonation, volume, visual aids and so on – to hit home your Core message.

The Crust: *holding it all together*

The Crust surrounding all of the content represents the style with which you deliver your content. This is where you pull together all five public speaking skills to create an inspiring message.

In the Crust you can write a few keywords to remind you of the decisions you have taken about how to behave as you speak. You might remind yourself of some of the following:

Authenticity: what is the real reason that I'm doing this?

Awareness: what features of my body and voice will I emphasise?

Empathy: what do my audience need from me?

Freshness: what do I want the audience to remember?

Balance: what are the key moments of impact in my structure?

Fearlessness: how does my stage persona want to behave?

Choose a few elements that are most important to your delivery. It could be that you write 'Big Bear' as the stage persona you want to unleash during your talk. Or you could colour the Crust in yellow, to represent the way you would like to speak to your audience. Do whatever works for you.

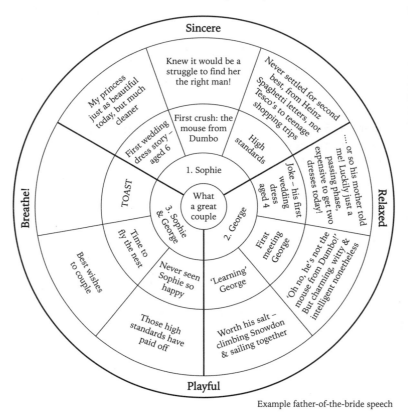

Example father-of-the-bride speech

The Content Pie and timing

As you'd expect, the more content you have, the more time you will need to deliver it. If your speaking time is cut or lengthened at the last minute, a Content Pie is an invaluable tool. Because of the visual format you can bulk up or slim down a talk at a moment's notice.

The layers of the pie help you to work out how much content you need to put in. Different content pies will take different amounts of time to deliver, depending on how much you talk around each point. But as a general guideline, you can expect the following time estimations if you spend some time with each point:

Core only: Up to 1 minute of speaking. This would be a very quick summary of a concept.

Core + 3 Themes: 30 seconds to 10 minutes. A short speech, should focus on getting across your themes. Of course, you can add a few vivid details to spice up each theme, as in the example of the father of the bride's speech on the previous page.

Core + 3 Themes + 9 Sections: 15 to 30 minutes. A presidential inauguration such as Obama's in 2009 might last 20 minutes and focus on broad, meaty sections, rather than using too many specific details.

Core + 3 Themes + 9 Sections + 27 points: 45 minutes+. A full Content Pie can suffice for a lengthy speech, through to a whole day of educational material, depending on how much time is spent on each detail. Just using a simple tool like the Content Pie, you can create a balanced and powerful experience for your audience.

The Content Pie and memory

A helpful by-product of making a Content Pie is that it helps you to commit your content to memory. Creating the Pie is in itself a method of 'chunking' – a term coined by George A. Miller in the 1950s to describe a way of grouping information into manageable units.

Whilst you're in the process of choosing the arguments that relate to your Sections and the Sections that relate to your Themes, you're already encoding information and connecting it together in a way that feels logical to you. So long as your logic holds, you don't need to remember anything ever again because if you get stuck, you just think about where the logic takes you. With your Content Pie built into your brain, all you have to remember is three simple groups of words at a time. Each three come logically from the one before. So long as you can remember your Core message, you can remember your Three Themes, your Sections and your arguments.

As body education expert Moshe Feldenkrais said, 'You can only forget things that you've remembered.' If you haven't remembered anything because your structure is logical and balanced, you can't forget anything. This is how some public figures step up on stage with no notes and still manage to say something sensible.

And, since you have created a structure that's neat and memorable for your audience, it will be equally neat and memorable for you.

What if . . . I'm a particularly forgetful person?

Expert tip: David Thomas

'The worst thing you can do to remember a speech is to sit down and try to memorise a pile of cue cards,' says World Memory record holder, David Thomas.

'As a memory champion, I can't get away with using notes when I speak in public. So I use the "journey technique" to accurately map out everything I say. It works like this:

1 Create a journey around a building you're familiar with, like your home. You're going to place a different stimulus at different points in your house to help you remember your lines.

2 Start with the front door. If your first message is about sales, imagine a big, white boat sail flapping in the wind at your door.

3 Next, you want to speak about performance, so you step into the front hall and there's Linford Christie warming up in lycra shorts, or a Ferrari, or whatever signals performance to you.

---

4 Keep going through all of the rooms of your house, adding the next part of your speech. The trick is to make each image ridiculous or fun. The more silly the image, the more you have an emotional response and the more you remember.

'Using this method, you can memorise 20 key words in just 12 minutes, which will give you 10 to 20 minutes of speech with no notes. If you forget what you're supposed to be saying, just go back into your house and find the next image.'

Balance workout

☐ **Design a compelling flow for your next talk.** Decide where the intensity of the talk should peak and choose techniques from the other chapters to build intensity.

☐ **Get a plot.** Choose a story-line for your talk; perhaps it will be a melodrama, a game of ping-pong, the tower or a plot of your own creation.

☐ **Find your core.** Brainstorm possible Core messages that are at the heart of your talk and test out a few on friends or colleagues. This is something that's worth getting right.

☐ **Design your next talk using the Content Pie.** Stick as much as possible to the suggested structure and see how it benefits your message. Does it make it clearer? More concise? Easier to remember?

☐ **Test your memory.** Once you're adept at using the Content Pie, forget about using notes altogether. If you've gone through the process carefully you'll have a mental map of your talk.

Part

5

There are only two types of speakers in the world.
1. The nervous and 2. Liars.

Mark Twain

Sonia Speakwell took a deep breath as she looked out to her crowd. They were beaming at her, but there was one final thing she wanted to do before they finished. Tell *her* story. Something clutched at her heart and she knew that was where her story had to come from.

She took one more breath, calmer this time, and started, 'I'd never been to Africa before . . .'

Fearlessness

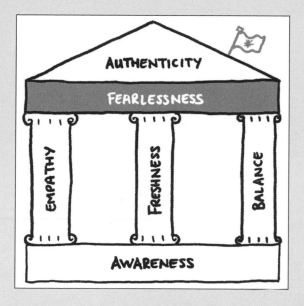

By developing a foundation of awareness and the three public speaking pillars you have mastered the art of doing a good job as a public speaker. Well done. But is 'good' enough?

The title of this book is *How to Be Brilliant at Public Speaking*. Which means becoming a speaker who can influence and inspire. And you'll do this by developing Fearlessness.

Take a look at those rare moments of passion when a speaker stands up and speaks from their heart. From Jesus to Gandhi, Abraham Lincoln to Mandela, these people have inspired and provoked social revolutions that have changed the world – and have gone down in history as some of the world's finest orators as a result.

But thousands of other, lesser-known speakers have spoken in a way that's as powerful as these famous speakers, or even more so. Fearless public speaking, more than any other communication method I know, has the capacity to change people on a profound level. It brings communities together; it forces difficult truths to be spoken; it captures the imagination of listeners; and it gives courage to others when they need it most.

Why would you settle for 'good' when your speech could move your audience to action around something that's important to you?

What is perfect Fearlessness?

- Stretching yourself, whatever your starting point, to be capable of more.
- Going beyond your comfort zone whenever it's beneficial.

- Doing whatever's necessary as a speaker to serve the needs of your audience.
- Enjoying making mistakes and learning from them.

Importantly, Fearlessness isn't about somehow destroying your fear, or suppressing it. We all feel fear (or nerves, or anxiety, or tension) to some degree before an important public speaking gig. Fearlessness is about transforming the energy of anticipation from fear to excitement.

As first suggested by William James in 1884, emotions are bodily experiences that we attach a certain meaning towards – like or dislike. When we look at it, we can see that fear and excitement are two sides of the same coin: fear is anticipating something negative and excitement is anticipating something positive. Anticipating something negative causes us to freeze, procrastinate and avoid. Anticipating something positive causes us to dive in.

That's why some people are drawn to rollercoasters, bungee jumping and mountain biking, whilst others presented with the same opportunity steer clear. Both parties experience a similar sensation of adrenaline entering their body, but their positive or negative anticipation determines whether or not they act.

Fearlessness, then, is about harnessing your fear and continuing to act, whether or not you feel afraid.

How do you develop Fearlessness?

This part will focus on two broad sections:

1. Understanding fear.
2. Tools for developing Fearlessness.

Chapter

9

Understanding fear

What is public speaking fear?

So many public speakers I work with are more afraid of being *afraid* than of the actual public speaking. They avoid public speaking because they imagine that all sorts of terrible things could happen if they're afraid. Cue visions of the ground opening up beneath you and swallowing you whole. In reality, there is a well-studied list of effects fear can have on you – and not one of them is the world ending. By understanding fear, you no longer need to be afraid of it.

Research into performance anxiety in music has shown that there are four state changes that fear can cause. You may experience all or some of these in varying degrees:

1. Emotion: Feeling nervous, stressed, worried or panicked.
2. Thought: Forgetting your words or losing concentration.
3. Behaviour: Trembling, fidgeting, moving in an awkward way.
4. Physiology: Upset breathing, faster heartbeat or an upset stomach.

By understanding that these are symptoms of public speaking fear, you can get distance from them. Next time you're asked to speak in public and you get an upset stomach, you can realise that it's a natural and common experience.

It's also heartening to know that you're not alone. Almost everyone experiences at least one of these state changes when they're preparing to speak – even the professionals. It's easy to think that you're the only one who gets nervous when all you see is other speakers giving confident performances. But remember that their fear may express itself in their worry before they start speaking, or their faster heartbeat that they've learned to control.

> ## What if . . . I'm too afraid to even try public speaking?
>
> *Expert tip: Lysette Offley*
>
> 'To have the courage to stand up and speak, you need to find what's really important to you about doing it,' says cognitive coach Lysette Offley of Sounds Positive. 'If you've conditioned yourself over many years to fear public speaking, you need to retrain your hardwiring to respond differently.
>
> 'Start this process by writing down a list of one hundred reasons why public speaking is important to you. This is a hell of a number, so you really have to go into depth. Look for reasons why it's important to your brain, your career, your personal development and so on.
>
> 'Writing the list brings the Reticular Activating System into play, which controls what we notice. You'll have experienced your RAS whenever you've bought a high price item like a car; suddenly everywhere you look is the same car. It also happens with a major life-changing experience – if you've just had a baby, are about to get married, or divorced, suddenly everywhere there are adverts, TV shows, conversations, books about that topic.
>
> 'In the same way, your hundred reasons stimulate the brain so that it can't help but notice all the benefits you'll get from public speaking. When that happens you'll develop the intention "I want, I want, I want" towards public speaking. Eventually you may find yourself moving heaven and earth just to be given a chance to speak!'

What's *my* public speaking fear?

Now let's examine your very own cocktail of fears that prevent you from expressing your full force as a speaker. One way to understand this is to map out the public speaking behaviours that you're currently capable of and to see which are currently beyond your grasp. This is your public speaking comfort zone.

Beyond your comfort zone is your fear zone: the areas of public speaking that you limit yourself from. These are the behaviours you might excuse as 'inappropriate' or 'not for me'. In most cases these limitations relate to some kind of fear that you hold inside, rather than what an audience will tolerate. Have you ever heard an audience ask a speaker to be more boring, less interactive or less memorable?

Have a look at the figure on p. 194 and ask yourself how courageous you are on each spectrum. Map your comfort zone by scoring yourself between 1 (not at all courageous) and 10 (perfectly courageous) for each element. Join the dots to see how big your comfort zone is right now. More on this is available in my website resources section – www.gingerpublicspeaking.com.

Map your comfort zone now.

1. Your Speaker's Toolkit

Think back to the Awareness chapter and all of those skills we looked at. How much work do you have to do to get to full courage with using powerful gestures, gaps, varying your volume, using movement and so on to engage your audience?

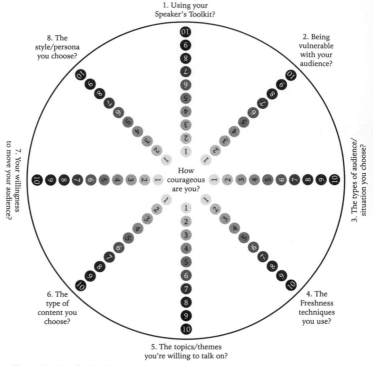

Public Speaking Comfort Zone Map

Mark your courage in each area – 10= perfect courage, 1 = not at all courageous – and connect the dots. This forms a map of your comfort zone with respect to public speaking.

2. Being vulnerable with your audience

How much do you give of yourself when you're speaking? Are you willing to share personal stories? Can you make mistakes and laugh at them along with the audience? Are you willing to let your full passion, fear, hurt or sadness show to the audience?

3. The types of audience or situation you choose

Are you comfortable speaking to any type of audience, in any situation, or do you have boundaries? Would you be willing to speak to CEOs? Children? Prisoners? Are you comfortable with small audiences? Audiences of hundreds? Thousands? Would your comfort zone stop at an after-dinner speech? A speaking competition? Speaking on TV?

4. The Freshness techniques you use

How many different techniques are you comfortable using to make your message memorable? Do you stick to your PowerPoint template, or are you willing to try interactive games, group work, video, props or role play? How willing are you to upset the usual routine?

5. The topics/themes you're willing to talk on

Do you have a set topic that you always talk on, or are you able to give impromptu speeches about almost anything? Within your topic, do you always rely on the same themes to talk around, or are you capable of mixing it up when beneficial?

6. The type of content you choose

Do you gravitate towards the same sort of content, or are you able to choose the most appropriate content for your speaking scenario? Are you comfortable with factual content? Discussion-led content? Inspirational content? With selling a concept or product? Do you adapt your content depending on whom you're speaking to, the room you're using and other environmental factors like outside noise, or do you stick rigidly to your planned content?

7. Your willingness to *move* your audience

How willing are you to create a change of mindset in your audience? Are you willing to request something of your audience? Could you break rapport to make an impact? Could you say 'no' to your group if need be? Could you tell them the tough truth? Are you willing to risk their dislike in the service of making a change?

8. The style/persona you choose

Do you always use the same personality style when you speak, or are you able to vary and flex your character, depending on who your audience are and what they need? Could you be excited? Enthusiastic? Serious? Silly? Profound? Relaxed? Challenging? Conciliatory? (See stage persona in Chapter 10 for advice about how to develop your Fearlessness in this area.)

Your Comfort Zone Map

Once you have drawn your Comfort Zone Map, take a step back and look at it. What do you notice about its size and shape? The top elements – 1, 2, 7 and 8 – relate to your personal power as a speaker and the bottom elements – 3, 4, 5 and 6 – are about the non-personal or environmental aspects of your public speaking.

Please note that the aim here is to map your comfort zone and zone of fear, nothing more. I'm not asking you to now speak to audiences that are irrelevant to you just to show you can, nor to embarrass yourself on an important occasion simply to show how fearless you are.

Rather, this exercise hopefully opens your mind to the idea that some behaviours which might be beyond your comfort zone right now may be just the thing you need to serve your audience more effectively, and therefore help you achieve your aims for public speaking. We'll look at practical methods for stretching out of your comfort zone later in this chapter.

This is an incredibly useful tool I use with my clients to establish how far they've come – and to congratulate them on that – and how far they still have to go to get to their full force as speakers.

Where does fear come from?

The Comfort Zone Map helps you understand your public speaking limitations and points towards your fears. But it doesn't explain the cause of those fears. Let's turn to the research to see various explanations for where fear of public speaking comes from.

Fear is often a complicated process to unpick, so the chances are your fear will be made up from a combination of these causes and perhaps experiences that are personal to you.

1. The perceived risk of speaking

Cognitive behavioural theory suggests public speaking is a type of social phobia. Researchers argue that an individual in part creates their social phobia by overestimating the likelihood and the consequences of their failure, or by perceiving public speaking to be riskier than it really is.

If you believe you're likely to fail, you will experience public speaking anxiety. Recent research shows that it's what we understand to be the consequences of failure that gets us most off-balance. We grossly exaggerate what's at stake with our public speaking.

These thoughts are often hidden somewhere, just below the rational surface of our mind. Even if we know our fears to be *logically* impossible, deep down we believe the risks to be genuine possibilities. Do any of these thoughts sound familiar?

If I mess up, I'll . . .

look like an idiot

ruin the whole event

get the sack

cause a major embarrassment to so-and-so

lose out on an opportunity permanently

Psychologists have classified these thoughts into five distinct fears of failure:

1. Fear of experiencing shame and embarrassment.
2. Fear of not meeting up to your own standards.
3. Fear of having an uncertain future as a result of your performance.
4. Fear of important others losing interest in you/what you're saying.
5. Fear of upsetting important others.

The more we focus on these possibilities, the bigger they become in our mind. Soon we see no other option than a dramatic failure and we'll do anything to get out of facing an audience.

Put differently, the risk of failure comes from taking yourself and your public speaking gig too seriously. If you see a particular moment of public speaking to be your *only* chance to succeed, you will see it as a very serious occasion indeed.

People around you will also contribute to intensifying the risk of a public speaking situation, perhaps due to their own vicarious fear. When you combine your own fear of failure with the fear of failure that others hold, the risks seem both very serious indeed and very likely to happen.

2. Focusing on yourself

Research shows a connection between the level of fear experienced and the amount a speaker focuses on themselves. This means that the more a speaker worries about *their* lines, *their* performance and *their* visual aids, the more anxious they will feel in comparison to speakers who focus on matters beyond personal aspects of the speaking assignment, as mentioned in the empathy chapter.

A more audience-focused speaker will notice that they are *not* the most important person in the room and that the people listening also have needs. This speaker's focus on the audience will lessen their anxiety because they have more important things to think about than themselves.

Focusing on yourself also makes you biased towards information that confirms your belief about yourself and your situation. As long as you focus on yourself, you'll find all the information you need to support the belief that you're messing up (perhaps the one person in the crowd who's looking bored) and you'll ignore every sign that you're doing well (the other 100 people who are listening intently). And, as research also shows, the more you focus on yourself, the less able you will be to speak well and the more likely it is that your performance will be poor. In this way we create our own vicious circles.

3. Perfectionism

A third source/cause of fear can be your personality type. I sometimes see nervous public speakers over-preparing for performances in a way that smells of perfectionism. Cognitive behavioural science has shown a connection between perfectionism and fear. Perfectionists who look to their audience to determine how well they did experience more anxiety.

If you have any of the following habits then you could be a perfectionist:

- Taking failure to heart.
- Ruminating over failure, even a long time after it has passed.
- Turning one failure, 'I failed on this occasion,' into a generalisation, 'I am a failure'.
- Treating ambiguous or neutral feedback as negative.

Perfectionists rely heavily on their success to feel a sense of self-worth, so if they fail or are worried that they will fail, they will experience a high degree of distress or anxiety.

4. Your self-talk language

We all have an inner dialogue going on almost constantly through our waking hours that tells us how we're doing in relation to the world around us. This is known by psychologists as 'self-talk'. Often, we aren't even aware of what we're telling ourselves, but it's still there, bubbling under the surface.

Research has shown that positive self-talk improves success in sports as varied as tennis, darts and figure skating and that negative self-talk reduces the chance of success. The same seems to be the case for public speaking.

Imagine the public speaker who steps on stage having spent the past two days thinking, 'I'm boring, I'll forget what I'm going to say, they won't like me.' How will his confidence be affected? His self-talk will affect his posture and the way he talks, so that the feedback he gets from his audience will reinforce his belief. 'That's why I'm afraid of public speaking', will be his triumphant declaration over a glass of whisky later that evening, 'I told you I was no good at it.' If he'd injected himself with sustained positive self-talk during the run-up to his talk, his experience may have been very different.

Another name for negative self-talk is the 'saboteur' or 'inner demon'. This is the part of our inner world where doubt, fear, criticism and vulnerability live. Our saboteur is the part of us who wants us to stop, go back, or hide in our comfort zone. He or she is the thought pattern that prevents us from expressing our full power as a speaker. To understand your fear, you should understand your saboteur. Ask yourself:

- What does your saboteur tell you about you and public speaking?
- What do they tell you you're incapable of?
- What behaviour do they warn you against?
- What does your saboteur tell you will happen if you make a mistake whilst speaking?
- If your saboteur were a person or character, what would they look like? Feel free to go crazy with the warts and green slime in your imagination. By creating an identity for your saboteur, you can start to show that you and your saboteur are not the same person.

The saboteur is nothing more than a habitual pattern of thought that takes too much control in certain life situations. We'll look at how to handle them in Chapter 10.

5. How you see yourself

Finally, your self-image also plays a role in building public speaking fear. Self-image is the mental picture you hold of yourself as a public speaker. Do you imagine yourself on stage as someone shining with confidence, or someone small and awkward-looking?

Speakers with high levels of anxiety are more likely to have a self-image that's negative and vague, in comparison to more confident speakers. They picture themselves as generally not that good at public speaking, but don't see the exact things that they're doing wrong (that's why Awareness is so important).

The crucial thing to remember is that your self-image isn't the same as how you actually come across to an audience. In my workshops I often watch speakers give a perfectly confident talk and then collapse back into their seats, complaining of how nervous they were and how terrible their performance was. Typically, the audience don't notice. Or if they do notice, they don't care all that much, so it doesn't affect their impression of you.

Where you view your self-image from is also important. Research shows that nervous public speakers are more likely than calmer ones to recall themselves speaking from outside their body looking in, rather than from inside their body looking out. It could then be possible that picturing yourself from outside the body plays a role in increasing public speaking fear.

If you don't want fear, what shall we have instead?

By now I hope you've understood something about what your particular cocktail of public speaking fear looks like and where it comes from. If you look back at the last section and compare the five different places fear comes from, you'll notice something striking:

Your evaluation of potential negative consequences;

Your self-focus;

Your perfectionism;

Your self-talk;

Your self-imagery

. . . all of these come from *you* and are maintained by *you*. In other words, you are the root cause of your public speaking fear.

It can be quite startling to realise that you cause your own fear. And it's really true. Who or what else is there to blame, when you can see that there are other people in the world who have managed what you're afraid to do? It can't be the case that any of your fears are being pumped into the air by a factory somewhere, or everyone would have them in equal portions.

In reality, this is good news. Because if you cause your own public speaking fear, you can also get rid of it too. No need to hunt down that fear factory. Now we can focus on changing fear into energy that benefits your message and your audience.

Chapter

10

Tools for developing fearlessness

Our aim is not to avoid or remove fear, but to take its energy and use it to benefit your performance. This is what I mean when I refer to Fearlessness.

So, in this chapter I'm going to give you the strategies that my clients and I have found to be most successful for transforming fear into Fearlessness.

Fearlessness Strategy 1: Change your mental imagery

In this strategy we'll use a Neurolinguistic Programming (NLP) tool to work with our senses to adjust the way we anticipate events.

Using this technique you can shift negative anticipation (fear) into positive anticipation (excitement) towards your public speaking assignment. Here's how to do it:

1. Close your eyes and allow your mind to drift towards your public speaking assignment.
2. Spend some time noticing what senses are stimulated. What do you see, smell, taste or hear, or what can you touch?
3. Gather this information and notice how it makes you feel on a bodily level. When we are anticipating something to be an unpleasant experience we tend to become tenser and our breathing and posture change.
4. Even if it is uncomfortable, spend some time experiencing this state and really noticing the senses that are activated

within you. This is a combination of all of your fears and expectations.

5. Now comes the fun bit. With every sensory impression you notice, you can shift it to become something else, simply by using your imagination. By playing with your mental imagery, you can unlock your fears on an unconscious level:

Image

- Are you watching yourself from the outside, or from inside your body? You are more likely to feel confident if you picture yourself from your body looking out.

- What sense of colour is there in the room? What happens to your fear if you make your picture more colourful? Brighter? Or black and white?

- Is your image clear or fuzzy? Sharpen your image and see which level of focus feels best.

- Do you see your audience as large and overpowering? Are they standing or sitting? Can you see their faces? Are they all around you, or far away? Adjust your audience until you feel powerful.

- Do you have particular types of people in your image of the audience? If you're nervously focusing on one important person in the audience, what would happen if you picture them with a clown's nose, or in a silly costume? What if you shrink them so that they're tiny?

Sound

- Can you hear yourself talking, or do you fail to fill the room? What happens if you turn up the volume of your voice?

- What reactions do you imagine hearing from your audience? Play with silence, laughter and fidgeting to see how it affects your confidence. Choose an audience that makes you feel wonderful about yourself.

- Try playing a soundtrack to your image. What happens if you speak to the *Indiana Jones* theme tune, or the *1812 Overture*?

Kinaesthetic

- What do you see yourself doing on stage? If it's tripping up, or another action that depletes your confidence, change what you see to something that brings you confidence.

- What temperature is it in your mental image? What happens if you turn the thermostat up, or down?

- How heavy do you imagine your body to be? Play with having a body that's as light as a balloon, or as heavy as a tree trunk.

- How does the floor feel – is it hard and businesslike, or soft and welcoming? If you want, you can speak from a grass platform, or a sandy beach – whatever makes you feel good.

6. Now that you've experimented with the senses in your mental imagery, it's time to lock them in. Set your mind on the most powerful elements of your mental image – these are two or three adjustments that bring you the most confidence.

7. Practise making these adjustments. Call to mind your original mental imagery, then make your changes. Make sure that they're big and obvious and make you feel great.

8. Keep practising this every time you think of your public speaking assignment. If you slip into your old mental image, play around with it again until it's once more fun and confidence-building.

Fearlessness Strategy 2: Visualise success

Visualising success is proven to work in reducing anxiety about public speaking and it brings you the courage to step well beyond your comfort zone. This strategy works on your self-talk to create an alternative outcome for your public speaking that fills you with positivity. The clever part is that whilst it tricks you into feeling more confident on the one hand, it also makes you more likely to succeed on the other, because your brain already thinks that you've got there. Therefore barriers in your way, like those pesky saboteurs, are reduced to dust.

To allow a visualisation to work effectively, you should come with an open mind and try not to control or force where your mind takes you. A visualisation is a chance to switch off your logical mind and tap into your subconscious.

As a result, visualisations work best if you have someone read them to you, so that you can close your eyes and listen. You can download a more in-depth audio version of this visualisation from my website, www.gingerpublicspeaking.com.

Alternatively, find a quiet space to read through the visualisation below, giving yourself plenty of time to sink into each stage of the process. It will take 10 to 20 minutes, so make sure you won't be interrupted. It's useful to keep a pen and paper handy, since the moment we relax thoughts can pop up that we don't want to forget. If that's the case, just write down 'Take dog for walk' so that you won't have to cling to the thought any more.

Confidence visualisation

1. Find yourself a quiet space where you won't be disturbed. Close your eyes if you like and start to focus on your breath, letting any nerves or panicked thoughts just drift by.

2. As you focus on your breath, imagine you're breathing in a colour you associate with confidence and breathing out a colour you associate with negativity.

3. Spend 5 to 10 minutes using this method to get into a state of confidence and positivity. Let your body shape change as you feel more confident. Your shoulders will come back and you'll be taller and more open.

4. Now, glowing with confidence, imagine yourself stepping into the room or onto the stage that you are speaking from. If you know what the room is like, move yourself there slowly and confidently, noticing all the details you can on the way. If you haven't seen the room before, just enjoy the sense that you're walking into a room that is filled with positive people.

5. Stand in front of your audience, taking a moment to enjoy the sensation of being the centre of attention. You notice that you're not daunted by the prospect of speaking. You feel confident, calm and supported by the audience. They can't wait to hear what you have to say and you can't wait to say it. Spend some time here, enjoying the moments before you start to speak. You may choose to look members of your audience in the eye, or to breathe in the atmosphere of the room. Do what it takes to get yourself feeling familiar and happy with your surroundings.

6. Now, as you start to speak, you find yourself whisked into the minds of the audience. You are now watching yourself speaking. You are amazed at how confident, how knowledgeable and how entertaining you are as a speaker. Take a moment to watch what it is that you're doing as a speaker to show that confidence. Is it in the way you walk? How you use your voice? How you interact with your audience?

7. Finally, as you start to wrap up what you have to say, you find yourself back in your own body. Your time in the public eye has gone better than you could've imagined. Look at all of the grinning faces and smiling eyes in the audience. And as you say your final words, your audience thank you for what you had to say. Do they cheer? Are they on their feet to applaud you? Are people rushing to congratulate you? What impact have your confident words had on your audience?

8. Soak up this feeling – this is your power as a speaker. It exists inside you, whether or not you've let it out so far.

9. Finally, take with you the feelings of calm and power that exist within your room and put them inside a part of your body where your confidence lives. This is usually your heart or your stomach. Know that all that confidence is there for you to access whenever you need it. And with that, you can gently come back to your present state and open your eyes.

Visualisations are useful tools to reprogramme the nervous parts of your mind. To benefit from the maximum impact, do this visualisation daily in the run-up to your big moment.

> ## What if . . . I panic?
>
> *Expert tip: Joan Bird*
>
> 'Breathing is crucial to overcoming panic,' says charisma coach Joan Bird, who has 30 years' broadcast journalism experience from both ends of the camera.
>
> 'One time I was presenting on *World News* and I got it in my head that the first story on the autocue wasn't the first story. I panicked and started to read the second story and the whole programme went into turmoil! If I had just breathed instead, I wouldn't have made a silly decision.
>
> 'Deep and coherent breathing stops the body from entering fight-or-flight mode. Practise before your speech by taking deep breaths and noticing the difference it makes – first to your physiology and then to your speech.
>
> 'When you're on stage, nobody will ever think your pauses are too long. In fact, if you take your time and breathe, they'll think you're more credible. Through practising breathing, I learned to trust myself and sound credible, even if when I don't feel it.'

Fearlessness Strategy 3: Ditch your saboteur

If your saboteur is really strong, they may block you from visualising success. This can come in the form of being unable to imagine the crowd feeling positive towards you, or it could be that your saboteur wants you to avoid trying the visualisation altogether. If this is the case, you'll need to find a mechanism for getting that saboteur under control. Here is a three-step process to do that:

1. Check the logic of the saboteur

Saboteurs only hold power when we know them to be true. Byron Katie has developed a highly effective method of questioning your thoughts, which applies to public speaking saboteurs. Take the saboteur's thought – for example, 'They won't like me because I'm not an interesting public speaker' – and ask yourself, 'Can I be 100 per cent sure this is true?' The answer can be either yes or no. Unless you can prove to yourself 100 per cent that you are not an interesting speaker (or whatever message it is that your saboteur is giving you), you will have to say 'No'. In this way, you begin to discredit your saboteur because their thought is no longer true in all situations.

2. Find replacement thoughts

Now that this saboteur's thought has been discredited, you'll want to find a more accurate thought to put in its place. Try substituting, 'They won't like me because I'm not an interesting public speaker' with thoughts that are:

Positive: What we tell ourselves becomes true, so we may as well tell ourselves positive things. Try substituting 'I'm not an interesting public speaker' with 'I have great insights about my topic' or 'I really care about my audience learning from me'. Find a thought that's positive and feels authentic.

Specific for negatives and general for positives: It can be useful to admit a mistake you made in a previous public speaking scenario to recognise the truth in what you're saying. Don't generalise this negative thought to yourself as a speaker. Keep any negative thoughts on the present time and situation, so you can see they aren't universal truths. Substitute 'I'm not an interesting speaker' for 'When I spoke in May, I wasn't as interesting as I would've liked to be'. When you use replacement thoughts that are positive, you can allow them to make general statements about who you are as a person or speaker: 'I am an interesting speaker' or 'I am enthusiastic about the topic.'

In your control: Base your thoughts around things that you are able to influence, rather than things that are out of your control. Your mental attitude and your preparation are in your control. Your audience's reaction, unforeseen distractions, mistakes and audio-visual problems are out of your control.

So, although 'They will like me!' is both positive and general, it isn't a useful replacement thought, because this isn't something you can control. It's only 'positive thinking' without a realistic chance of success. If you finish your 'They will like me!' talk feeling that your audience didn't like you, your saboteur will come back stronger than ever with 'I told you so'. Instead, form a replacement thought such as 'I will be happy with whatever I manage' or 'I will like myself whatever happens'.

3. Say 'thanks and goodbye' to the saboteur

Now that you have a replacement thought, you no longer need your saboteur's advice. Yet the saboteur will often pop up when you least expect them to offer an unhelpful message. When this happens you'll know because it feels like your energy has been dragged downwards. To kick your saboteur out once and for all, develop a 'break mechanism' to cut off the saboteur's power. A break mechanism is a trigger to help you switch off the saboteur as soon as you notice you're under their influence. Using your characterisation of your saboteur (see p. 200), try these break mechanisms:

- Imagine your saboteur shrinking in size to a tiny dot. As they shrink, hear their voice getting quieter and quieter, so that all you're left with is silence and calm.

- Imagine yourself picking up your saboteur and unceremoniously dropping them into the bin, out of the window or off a really high bridge. Enjoy the feeling that they've left you for good.

- Use the NLP technique explained earlier (see p. 205) to ridicule the characterisation of your saboteur. Identify which features currently give the saboteur power over you. It may be their serious nose, tight lips, grey outfit or authoritative voice. Instead, give them a huge round nose and enormous lips, turn them fuchsia pink and change their voice to animal noises. Be creative and cheeky. The more ridiculous your saboteur looks, the more laughable they become.

Be persistent with your saboteurs. They have been with you for most of your life, so don't fret if they keep coming back. Know that each time you use your break mechanism, the saboteur loses power.

Fearlessness Strategy 4: Adopt a stage persona

Ewan McGregor has said that although he's perfectly happy to act on stage, he finds public speaking as himself '*horribly nerve-wracking and difficult*'. A way to handle this is simply not to go on stage as yourself. A stage persona acts as a protective mask for your ego. If you make a mistake in a stage persona, it isn't *you* exactly who makes the mistake, it's a character you're playing. This allows you not to take mistakes so personally, which in turn gives you the opportunity to act outside your comfort zone. You too can give a more fearless performance because there's nothing to risk – you're just acting a part.

What is a stage persona?

A stage persona is a collection of elements of your performance that your audience come to know and love you for, no matter what the context. For many professional speakers this is a particular style, such as humourous, informative or inspirational, which is combined with certain words, gestures and choices of style. We know what we're getting with Tony Robbins or Tony Blair because of their stage persona, or public image. Let's look at a process for developing your stage persona.

1. Work out your personal impact

What impact do you want to have on your audience to make your core message hit home? Do you want to be the speaker who entertains, informs or persuades? Professional speakers use one predominant stage persona, so I invite you to do the same.

Consider the six archetypes of public speakers below. Which 'hero' are you currently? Which would it *most benefit your message for you to be?* Which feels most authentic to you and your purpose? When designing your stage persona, stretch yourself to find a role that feels right for you, but that also feels aspirational and perhaps even scary. It's by choosing big shoes to fill that we grow to fit them faster.

Are you the Wizard, the Jester or the Monarch?

Sage: Hero of Information.

Focus: informing.

Influences by: giving the audience the answer.

Typically seen in: a lecture, factual workshop/class or general announcements.

The Sage is not afraid to give facts to her audience. She presents information in a way that is interesting, easy to understand and progresses the audience's intellectual understanding of a topic. It's thrilling to listen to her because the audience feel their intellectual needs are being met.

Jester: Hero of Laughter.

Focus: entertaining.

Influences by: making the audience laugh.

Typically seen in: a best man's speech, after-dinner speech or Christmas party toast.

The Jester distinguishes himself by making the audience smile, laugh or generally feel good. This releases endorphins into the body and makes the audience remember good times when they think of his message. As such, he focuses on the emotional needs of the audience.

Monarch: Hero of Power

Focus: assuring/asserting.

Influences by: showing the audience they're safe.

Typically seen in: a business or group leader's presentation or a politician's speech.

The Monarch is a commanding presence on stage, whether demanding we do better or offering congratulations. The Monarch is centred, focused, powerful and in charge. She creates her impact by being immovable and creating a 'rock' to rely on, satisfying the security needs of the audience.

Wizard: Hero of Transformation.

Focus: persuading.

Influences by: changing the audience's perspective.

Typically seen in: sales presentations, educational workshops or a persuasive speech.

The Wizard transforms cynics into believers and the disengaged into advocates. He connects with the audience by understanding what drives them and speaking their language. He gives just enough information to leave them wanting more.

Muse: Hero of Creativity

Focus: rousing innovation.

Influences by: encouraging the audience to think and act differently.

Typically seen in: a motivational speech, telling a personal story or a facilitated workshop.

The Muse acts as an example to the audience, to encourage them to discover, play and create. Pulling on the audience's discovery needs, she questions, teases or shows new ways of thinking.

Peacemaker: Hero of Care.

Focus: connecting.

Influences by: connecting the audience.

Typically seen in: facilitated group discussions, a leaving speech, or when acting as master of ceremonies.

The Peacemaker is a subtle yet powerful force in a room. His audience will leave feeling 'Weren't we great' rather than 'Wasn't he great' because of his ability to turn the spotlight on the audience. He connects the dots between topics, themes and feelings in the room and satisfies the audience's need to be nurtured or recognised.

Base your stage persona on the character you'd like to portray, not on the topic of the speech you're about to deliver. If you're a natural humorist, you'll feel comfortable using the Jester stage persona to deliver a best man's speech. However, many of us aren't authentic Jesters, which is why wedding speeches that contain 'forced humour' can nosedive. If you are a Peacemaker, there's no need to try to be a Jester because you've been asked to deliver that best man's speech. Instead, deliver a speech that tenderly connects you, the couple and the audience. This will feel much more authentic to you and your audience, so you'll all enjoy it more.

Design your stage persona using Appendix 4 (p.246).

What if . . . I'm not a very charismatic person?

Expert tip: Caroline Goyder

'While it's true that some people naturally have bucketloads of charisma, and some don't, everyone can shine in front of an audience,' says Caroline Goyder, author of *The Star Qualities: Sparkle with Confidence in All Aspects of Your Life.* 'Think of all the actors and comedians who are shy off-stage and switch it on in the spotlight. Cate Blanchett calls it "turning the lights on" and says she learned it at drama school.

'Turning the lights on is simple: you shine when you talk about someone you love, or something you are passionate about, or when you laugh. You focus your energy out on other people rather than into your worries or insecurities. It's the power of that generous feeling that gives you a glow and a sparkle. So, if you want to shine in front of an audience you have to make the audience feel something, and you do that by feeling something strongly yourself.

'To help this along, try George Clooney's trick of seeing the audience as old friends, so you relax, smile and sparkle. If all else fails, try the old actor's trick of having a naughty thought or a great secret – it works brilliantly for Johnny Depp!'

2. Choose the qualities of your stage persona

There aren't just six types of speaker out there – there are limitless possibilities. So once you have chosen a broad hero role that suits your personality and your message, start to add the colour.

What type of Sage, Monarch or Jester are *you*? Think of people you have admired in your life. Which of their qualities would you like to integrate into your stage persona? Would you like to have the warmth of George Clooney? The crisp cool of Judy Dench? The passion of Martin Luther King? Take these qualities and make your own inspiring list of how you want to behave whilst speaking in public.

You can also draw inspiration from nature to create your persona. Be creative. In the role of Monarch, are you a lion with a powerful roar but gentle strength? Or are you more of a silverback gorilla with his blunt force and gruff manners? Are you a Peacemaker, like a butterfly, darting gently in between different parties with grace and energy? Perhaps your butterfly has fangs when you need them? Or are you more of a cat who settles down with one member of the audience and spends time making them feel good, before moving on?

Start to create an image of your stage persona from these details.

3. Choose your 'trademark' features

Now that you know *who* your stage persona is, it's time to transfer that to how you behave on stage. What do you with your body, voice and words to be that butterfly with fangs? Again, design your trademark features based on who you want to be, rather than on what you currently feel you are capable.

If you think again of Tony Robbins and Tony Blair, they each have unique ways of using their Speaker's Toolkit to bring their stage persona alive. Tony Blair as Prime Minister played the Monarch, using his distinctive smile, expressive eyebrows and definite hand gestures, in combination with powerful use of gaps and quotable sound bites, to assert and assure. Tony Robbins plays the Wizard. He persuades his audience by offering fast-paced information, moving about the stage in a leonine fashion and using expressive gestures as if swishing his tail. His trademark with live audiences is to ask them to interact by 'Say[ing] Aye!' if they agree with what he's saying.

Develop your own trademark features. Perhaps your butterfly is light on her feet, uses gentle, lifting gestures and speaks softly. When the fangs come out, perhaps that's the moment of passion, volume and assertive body language, where she draws insight from a point that's come from the audience. Remember that your trademark features should always feel authentic to you, even if they're scary to implement at first.

4. Give your stage persona a name

Having a stage persona name helps you to step into character. For many years I characterised myself as the 'Energiser Bunny' on stage and would ensure that everything I said and did reinforced that character. With a name, you can think 'What would Dangerous Dave dress like?', or 'What would the Passionate Queen have to say if she were designing this talk?'

5. Give yourself permission to be a stage persona

Some people dislike public speaking precisely because it feels fake to play a character on stage. If that's you, you may feel uncomfortable about creating a stage persona for yourself. I hope you see by now that a stage persona isn't fake; it comes from bringing out your authentic inner qualities. It can feel funny to do anything that's not your usual behaviour, but if you want to improve your public speaking, you'll need to step outside your comfort zone.

Give yourself permission to get into your stage persona by remembering that this is in the service of a higher purpose; you want to achieve something as a result of speaking and a stage persona can help you get there by strengthening your Fearlessness. Remember that a stage persona is useful because public speaking is *necessarily* different from speaking one-to-one. You wouldn't use the same volume, speed of talking or word choice in a one-to-one conversation as you would speaking to an audience. They wouldn't hear you for starters. So, every time you are speaking in public you *are* adopting a stage persona, no matter how different you feel from your usual self. Logically, then, you may as well take control and assume your full force as a public speaker by adopting a stage persona.

6. And . . . Action!

Becoming Fearless happens when you take action, not when you're *thinking about* acting. So get out there and practise your new stage persona before the *really* important moment happens. By practising, you'll gain feedback on how powerful your stage persona is. See how far you can push it when you're in a low-risk situation, then you'll be able to transfer *at least* a diluted version of that power when it really matters.

If you struggle with motivating yourself into action, you're not alone. We secretly like holding onto our public speaking fear, because it means we don't have to act. Like skydiving, public speaking is possible to avoid. Unlike skydiving, sooner or later an opportunity will arise when it would benefit you to speak in public – and to do it well.

Get motivated to battle through your comfort zone before it's urgent. Remember your authentic reason for speaking that we identified at the start of this book. What do you want more than your fear of public speaking?

What if . . . I don't have anywhere to practise?

Expert tip: Roger Harding

'As a military man, I thought that I had understood fear,' says Roger Harding, public speaker and former President of Early Bird Speakers Toastmasters group. 'I've been shot at by East German border guards, blown up by the IRA, survived a Himalayan avalanche, even been charged by Tanzanian elephants.

'But when I joined a networking group where every week I had to stand up and speak in public for 60 seconds, I discovered a terrifying fear of public speaking. I wondered how I could get through it and started looking for somewhere to practise. I started going to a Toastmasters club – a structured public speaking club where people of all levels and backgrounds practise and receive feedback on their public speaking. I remember listening to more experienced speakers, even novices, at the group and thinking, "I can never be as good as them". Yet the group atmosphere creates confidence and demolishes nerves and fear.

'Five years on, I see the dramatic effects that Toastmasters can have on self-confidence and personal pride. Anyone can join and the groups are all over the country. Because of Toastmasters, I now list professional speaking on my CV.'

Fearlessness workout

☐ **Find out your public speaking comfort zone using the map tool in Chapter 9.** This will help you reflect on how far you've come as a speaker and how to step further into Fearlessness.

☐ **Learn where your fear of public speaking comes from.** See which of the causes of public speaking fear apply to you.

☐ **Pick the most appropriate fear-fighting techniques for you and put them into action.** Record your favourite tips in the Ingredients List on p. 241.

☐ **Adopt a stage persona for yourself.** Are you a Monarch, a Jester, a Sage or a Wizard? Aspire towards a character that feels authentic to you and would also benefit your audience. Use the 'Adopt a stage persona' resource (p. 213–217) to help you.

☐ **Practise!** Find somewhere you can get regular practice and feedback in front of an audience. Try a Toastmasters club near you, or find out about my public speaking programmes at www.gingerpublicspeaking.com.

Part

At the centre of your being you have
the answer; you know who you are and
you know what you want.

Lao Tzu

Wendy Wobbletalk felt a lump in her throat. She hadn't realised her boss would be watching her talk. Her stomach started churning.

'Oh no, he won't think I'm professional enough,' she found herself thinking. 'Maybe I should cut out the ice-breaker, or speed the discussion up a bit.' She fumbled with her PowerPoint clicker. 'Welcome to my projector,' she said, then blushed. 'Um, I mean, welcome to my presentation.' A few members of the audience folded their arms.

'Um,' she said apologetically. 'I . . . I'll just tell you a few things. . . I . . . um, won't be long.'

Authenticity

And now we have come full circle back to Authenticity. In this final part we'll investigate how to put Authenticity into action.

Without the other five elements of the Public Speaking House, Authenticity would be possible, but not powerful. Imagine a speaker who gushes from the heart, but in doing so uses dozens of 'ums', talks for far too long and forgets to say the things the audience wanted to hear. The audience may sympathise with them as a person, but their speaking will have limited power.

Likewise, a speaker who is Aware, Empathetic, Fresh, Balanced and Fearless can still lose their audience by coming across as false.

Authenticity is your chance to say powerfully, 'This is who I am, this is what I believe in and I will not budge from my message'. It enables you to engage with your audience, who will be persuaded to take on your message. Authenticity, then, is an important cherry on your public speaking cake.

However, in moments of panic, as with Wendy Wobbletalk earlier, it's easy to lose confidence in yourself. Suddenly your relaxed, authentic self is nowhere to be seen.

Chapter

11

It ends with authenticity

How we lose our authenticity

You enter a speaking scenario with certain assumptions. Assumptions of how you will behave, assumptions of how your audience will behave and assumptions of how your surroundings and equipment will behave. These assumptions prop up your ability to be your relaxed, confident self. When something goes wrong we become panicked and step into 'coping' behaviours that don't reflect our real, authentic selves.

For example:

'I'm expecting 30 people, who I hope will be polite and well-mannered. I have my speech prepared, I've timed it to exactly 10 minutes. My notes are in my back pocket just in case and I've practised using my props. What could possibly go wrong?'

This speaker's confidence is being propped up by the number of people in his audience, by their good manners, by his estimated timing, his back-up notes and his props.

Should a couple of his assumptions be bent, he may be able to adapt and retain his authenticity. For example, if only 15 people show up instead of the 30, he may be OK.

But if enough of these assumptions snap – meaning that the situation suddenly and dramatically changes – he may be thrown off-centre. There are so many things that could trigger this, such as tripping over as he comes to the stage, or an audience member asking an aggressive question he wasn't expecting.

If he's not careful, these snapped assumptions will lead to panic and he'll find himself pretending to be serious or important; waffling when he could just stay silent; or pretending to know the answer to a difficult question.

How to build authenticity

To express authenticity requires you to feel confident and stable in yourself. This is the state we know as being 'centred'. When you're centred, you have no need for worrying or second-guessing because you are simply present in the moment, acting authentically and doing whatever is necessary.

From your calm centre, you start to discover how much power you have as a speaker.

In our earlier example, Wendy Wobbletalk, an experienced speaker, loses her authenticity because of making a mistake. Unfortunately this happens to speakers all the time. Authenticity is about learning how to remain in your centre, no matter what happens to put you off. In the excitement of preparing a talk, this 'inner' preparation is almost always forgotten.

I'll now share some techniques for staying centred, which will help you come back to your authentic state whenever you need it.

1. Manage your assumptions

Prepare yourself by noticing the assumptions that form the foundations of your success. These are the safety blankets that you rely on – so long as they're there, you feel balanced. Remove a safety blanket and you feel less able to perform.

What and who are you relying on to ensure you're successful?

Are you secretly banking on:

- Your audience being of a certain age (. . . *then I'll impress them*)?
- A particular knowledge level (. . . *then my content will work*)?
- A certain room layout (. . . *then I'll be able to do this exercise, which will make them enjoy the talk*)?
- Being able to use particular equipment (. . . *then I'll look good*)?

Shine a light on all the safety blanket thoughts you might be whispering to yourself, like: 'I'm fine so long as the audience aren't too knowledgeable', or 'I really hope my boss isn't there.'

Once you've noticed these assumptions, you have a choice:

1. Hold fast to your safety blankets and do everything you can to manipulate your external environment, so that you won't have to face something that puts you off-balance.

2. Learn how to become a Weeble – one of those toy clowns with a rounded bottom. No matter how hard you push it, it will always come back to balance upright at its centre. A Weeble adapts to changing circumstances without being thrown.

As long as you lay your foundations for success in conditions that you can't control, you're setting yourself up for a wobbly ride. Surprises are inevitable in public speaking, because you have an audience with a will of their own. So, rather than fighting a losing battle to control the uncontrollable, strengthen your calm core by laying your foundations for success in yourself.

2. Becoming a Weeble

Step 1: Find your confidence within

Collect evidence that that you will do a good job, no matter what happens. Find confidence in:

- Your own experience in the subject matter. What knowledge or unique angle do you have that won't disappear, no matter how well the talk goes?

- Your ability to succeed. Think about all the times when you've succeeded in something, whether it's public speaking, or a related challenge from a different part of your life. Notice that even if things go wrong, at your core is someone who can – and does – succeed.

- How you shine when you're at your most comfortable. There's not a person in the world who isn't fun, interesting and inspirational when they're around their closest friends. This is the core of who you are, irrespective of what happens when you're speaking.

Step 2: Let disturbances pass

As mentioned in the Fearlessness chapters, when we feel socially anxious, we tend to judge feedback we receive more harshly. Reduce the impact of unexpected circumstances by practising allowing them to pass without reacting. After all, there's no such thing as an objectively bad event, only your interpretation of it. As much as it might seem like you have an evil laptop and projector that refuse to cooperate with you, the failure of your equipment is not objectively bad, it's you who can choose to make it so. If you allow your authentic self to act, you could choose to let the disturbance of the failed projector pass and see it as an opportunity to try something different with your audience.

Knowing that you should let disturbances pass is different to being able to do it. To train yourself, try mindfulness meditation, which has been shown to reduce stress and increase self-esteem.

Mindfulness meditation means simply watching your thoughts come and go, without following them. You can practise it by:

- Finding yourself a quiet spot to sit in for 10 minutes a day in the lead-up to your big talk.
- Aiming to sit and be present in the moment and to let any thoughts of past or future just go by.
- Not stopping, controlling or restricting thoughts – simply letting them pass without judging.

With patience and time, you will learn to distance yourself from disturbing thoughts so that you don't get knocked so far off-course when difficulties arise. You can access your centred, Weeble state in the middle of public speaking, simply by pausing and focusing on your breath.

Step 3: When you become derailed

But what if you can't just move on? Perhaps you've gone blank, or are blushing violently. What can you do to get back to your centre quickly? Here are some emergency methods:

1. **Take a sip of water:** This is normal behaviour for a speaker, so your audience will have no idea you've slipped up. A sip of water forces you to breathe and allows you to gain the space to step back into your centre.

2. **Change your posture:** Notice how you tighten up when you lose your centre. This is your body's reaction to embarrassment. Become aware of that and shift your posture to how you stand when you're feeling completely at ease. The shift in posture gives the brain a signal to shift emotional state.

3. **Call for someone else's input:** If appropriate, ask the audience a question or a colleague to comment, to give yourself time to regroup.

4. **Laugh!** There's no audience in the world who want to see you struggle, so if everything goes wrong, just look on it with humour. This is often the most authentic reaction to a problem and it will help your audience see you as a real person.

What if . . . I blush violently when I speak?

Expert Tip: Mindy Gibbins-Klein

'Rather than getting self-conscious if you blush, treat it as a gift,' says Mindy Gibbins-Klein, founder of The Book Midwife®. 'Instead of trying to ignore the elephant in the room, look for the positives.

'Blushing could put members of your audience at ease because they recognise that you're human too. Or, you could turn your blushing to your advantage by making reference to it in a way that's light-hearted and supports your message, e.g. *"If I go red, that just means you must all be on fire!"*

'I have massive hair, so when I speak it often gets in the mic. I mention it and use it to my advantage. The important thing is to focus on what you can control. You may not be able to control your blushing, or your hair, but you can control your reaction to it.'

Going beyond: The power of Authenticity

The very best speakers are not those who have the biggest audiences or the grandest salaries. The best speakers are those who touch their audience on a profound level because of their ability to fully unleash their authenticity. These speakers are able to act in a way that's beyond personal. They forget themselves and their nagging worries as a speaker and completely focus on what the audience – and that moment – need. If you're truly authentic, you're able to access whatever state is needed because you know it's beneficial. You can risk the discomfort, or disagreement, of the audience in the service of the higher purpose. Here's where truly powerful speaking lives.

Notice that authenticity isn't about expressing every emotion you happen to feel. 'Indulgent' authenticity risks damaging the Empathy pillar. For example, telling your 'idiot' audience just how frustrated you are with them could damage the group dynamics. However, if used to benefit the audience, your frustration could be just the trigger needed to make a breakthrough in their learning or their willingness to change. If you are aware and empathetic, you will gain a sense of when to express yourself fully.

On a practical level, authentic expression means any behaviour that serves the audience. To illustrate this, I'll show you how switching styles creates impact in your speaking.

Consider what happens when a Comic Relief comedian stops telling jokes and speaks from the heart about his experience of Africa. Or when a softly spoken mother stands up at a PTA meeting and demands from *her* heart that other sources of funding are found for her child's school. This power comes from using contrasting parts of your performance to impact your audience. It is a contrast that shocks and inspires at the same time. As we see from the millions raised by Comic Relief every few years, switching styles really has the power to change behaviour.

How do I switch my style?

From Chapter 10, you should know something about your preferred stage persona. Now, notice more about your typical style as a speaker. Is it your habit automatically to tell a joke? Do you jump straight into the details? Are you the 'excited' speaker? Are you only comfortable when you're in dialogue with your audience?

Chose a contrasting part of your personality to bring into your speaking when you need to influence or inspire (often when you're reaching the peak in intensity of your talk – see p.158). This is likely to be a part of the Authentic you that you normally keep tucked out of sight. Because it is less practised than other parts of your stage persona, it will come across to the audience as exceedingly Authentic.

These are some combinations that work well together:

- **Information versus reflection:** If you're a speaker who uses a lot of information or a very persuasive message, balance that power by switching into a mode that's much more gentle, reflective and spacious. Although it may feel uncomfortable to stop and leave white space for you and your audience to think, it could be just what they need to let your point sink home.

- **Humour versus sincerity:** Perhaps you've just delivered an entertaining wedding speech. You have your audience rolling in the aisles. You could leave it at that, or you could pause for a second and say, *'But in all seriousness . . .'* Switching to a sincere or even serious moment after you've had the audience laughing will bring them powerfully down to earth in a way that they'll remember. This is how comedies such as *Cold Feet* and *Scrubs* manage to create their most heart-wrenching moments.

- **Energy versus calm:** Everyone loves an energetic presenter, but if you're at the same energy level for your whole talk, you're missing an opportunity to impact your audience. Create balance by putting some moments of calm into your talk. This could be physical stillness as well as speaking in a calmer fashion. This contrast will further emphasise the power of your energy, whilst giving it a few moments to sink in. Likewise, if you're a typically calm presenter, challenge yourself to inject a burst of energy to show the audience key moments of passion or enthusiasm.

- **Mr Nice Guy versus Mrs Hard Nose:** If you are more naturally drawn to discussion in speaking, regularly seek affirmation from your audience, or look to create consensus in the room, you could be a Mr Nice Guy speaker. Don't get caught up in the need to be liked by everyone in your audience. This will make you mild, but not inspirational. Balance your Mr Nice Guy, which will win you friends in the audience, with Mrs Hard Nose. These are moments of 'telling it how it is' where you don't apologise, edit or moderate what you're saying:

  Mrs Hard Nose: 'This is bad.'

  Mr Nice Guy: 'Sorry to say, but it's not really all that good, I don't think.'

  This style switch, used wisely, will call your audience to action. They will like and respect you even more as a result.

To switch your style takes courage as you're often breaking the rapport that you have worked so hard to build. Rapport is only useful if you use it to create an impact. If you avoid breaking rapport, you are pulling away from your full power as a speaker.

The great majority of public speakers-in-waiting pull away from their power because they're unaware they can move an audience. 'Who am I to make people laugh and cry?' 'Who am I to be a catalyst?' 'Who am I to be a speaker who changes people's lives?'

As Marianne Williamson said, 'Who are you not to be?'

In fact, all you have to do is not actually to 'do' anything. It's to *be*. It's to be Authentic.

Authenticity workout

☐ **Notice what assumptions you're basing your success upon.** Write a list of all of the things that, under the surface, you need to have happen to be comfortable in public speaking. Prepare yourself – how will you stay balanced if each, or all, of these assumptions snap?

☐ **Learn to balance your state by trying the mindfulness meditation.** Become a Weeble by learning to let disturbances pass without being affected by them.

☐ **Investigate your Authentic posture.** How do you hold yourself when you're at your most relaxed and confident? Become aware of how you feel – in your shoulders, legs, stomach and so on. This is your centred state. When you get knocked off-centre, come back to this physical state by inviting each part of your body to relax.

☐ **From your balanced state, push yourself to become a powerful, inspiring speaker.** Try switching to the opposite style you're used to in order to make your maximum impact.

The road ahead

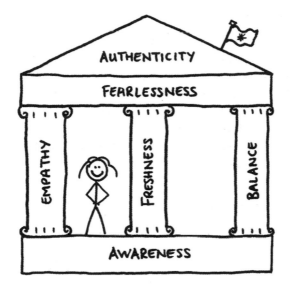

You now have everything you need to become a brilliant public speaker.

By sharpening your Awareness, you have built an unshakeable foundation from which to analyse your abilities as a speaker – a skill that will help you learn from any and every speaker you encounter as an audience member.

As an Empathetic speaker you will continue to speak to the audience's needs and benefit from their high regard for you as a result. With Freshness, you can use innovations to turn any public situation into one that's unique and memorable. And with Balance, you can put those innovations into a structure that makes sense for your audience and for you.

By reading this book you have already begun to strengthen your layer of Fearlessness and I hope that moving forwards you'll challenge yourself to step still further beyond your comfort zone in the service of your audience's needs.

Finally, with a new understanding of why public speaking is important to you and how to speak as the *real* you, I hope that you will feel inspired to unleash your Authenticity on audiences far and wide.

Remember that public speaking is a journey that takes time and the continued desire to improve. The best thing I can advise is for you to practise your speaking as often as possible, whilst adding to your skills set. My company, Ginger Training & Coaching, offers bundles more resources to help you on that journey, including a number of freebies that directly relate to this book. Head over to www.gingerpublicspeaking.com to take your next steps.

Appendix 1

Public Speaking Ingredients List

Use this space to record the tips from each chapter that you'd like to use in your public speaking:

Awareness – Using your Body and Voice for impact
Empathy – Audience-focused Preparation and handling difference audience types

Freshness – Vibrant Visuals, Wonderful Words and Ingenious Interactives to use

Balance – Key tips for creating internal and external balance

Fearlessness – Favourite techniques for stepping beyond your comfort zone

Appendix 2

The Um Game

Become aware of your 'ums' and 'erms' by playing the Um Game.

You'll need: two or more players, a stopwatch and strips of paper with words to guess written on one side. You could also use word cards from games like 'Taboo' or 'Articulate'.

Aim: Each player should try to get the others to guess as many words as possible.

Rules: Each player has 30 seconds per turn.

Your turn ends immediately if:

- You say the word on the card.
- You say 'um', 'erm' or any other filler (you can include 'basically', 'essentially' and so on if you like).
- ADVANCED RULES: Your turn ends if you gesture.

It's the audience's responsibility to point out any 'ums' or gestures.

Keep a count of any words that are successfully guessed.

Once your 30 seconds ends, or you make a mistake, pass the cards to the next person for their turn.

Give each player at least two or three turns to see how they improve as their awareness grows. This is a fantastic game to shine a light on your habits.

After you play the Um Game you may become acutely aware of your 'ums'. This is all part of the learning pathway (see learning pathway on p.xiv) – you're moving from *Blissfully Unaware* to *Rude Awakening*. But don't worry, after a while you'll learn to tame your 'ums'.

Appendix 3

Wonderful Words Bingo

Use this game of bingo to help you expand your range of Wonderful Words for your next public speaking encounter. Find a good example to fill each box, using the principles described on pp.113–120. Make a horizontal, vertical or diagonal line of four to prepare for a short speech, or get a full-house to be prepared for anything.

Title of speech/talk:			
Anchor Word	Joke/Humour	Evocative Image	Strong Fact
Song	Storytelling	Powerful Quote	Analogy
Strong Fact	Powerful Three	Famous Example	Poem
Joke/Humour	Metaphor	Anchor Phrase	Evocative Image

Appendix 4

Design your stage persona

Name:	
Archetype (Jester, Sage, Muse, etc.):	
Character qualities (warm, loud, fearless, etc.):	
What can your stage persona do that you wouldn't?	
How does your stage persona typically use body and voice?	
How do they use language?	
How do they dress?	
How else does your audience know you're 'in character'?	

Appendix 5

Further resources

I've put together a website with a wealth of resources to support you on your public speaking journey. Head over to www.gingerpublicspeaking.com for:

- Your free public speaking email coaching based around the 'Ginger Doodle' illustrations in this book. You'll receive 50 beautiful doodles and 50 public speaking tips over 50 days.
- Interviews with public speaking experts.
- Online workshops to help you overcome public speaking fear and strengthen all parts of your performance. Recommended if you want to take the lessons from this book further.
- Access to upcoming workshops from Ginger Training & Coaching, open to all aspiring speakers. If you're serious about becoming a brilliant speaker, these are not to be missed.
- Details of how to find me on Twitter and Facebook.

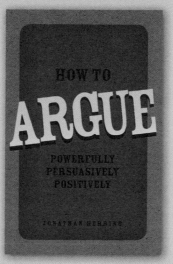
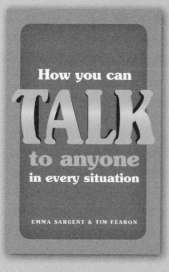
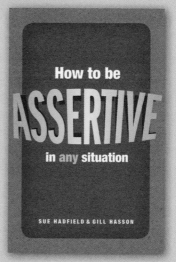